Collins

Cambridge IGCSE™

Physics

WORKBOOK

Gurinder Chadha

William Collins' dream of knowledge for all began with the publication of his first book in 1819.
A self-educated mill worker, he not only enriched millions of lives, but also founded a flourishing publishing house.
Today, staying true to this spirit, Collins books are packed with inspiration, innovation and practical expertise.
They place you at the centre of a world of possibility and give you exactly what you need to explore it.

Collins. Freedom to teach.

Published by Collins
An imprint of HarperCollins*Publishers*
The News Building, 1 London Bridge Street, London, SE1 9GF, UK

HarperCollins*Publishers*
Macken House, 39/40 Mayor Street Upper, Dublin 1, D01 C9W8, Ireland

Browse the complete Collins catalogue at
collins.co.uk

© HarperCollins*Publishers* Limited 2024

10 9 8 7 6 5 4 3 2 1

ISBN 978-0-00-867087-0

Acknowledgements
With thanks to the following teachers for reviewing materials and providing valuable feedback: **Frank Akrofi**, The Roman Ridge School; **Samuel Yeboah**, AVES International Academy; **Dr Raul Balbuena**, Tama Rama Intercultural School; **Dr Rahul Sharma**, IRA Global School; **Dániel Szücs**, International School of Budapest; and with thanks to the following teachers who provided feedback during the development stages: **Shalini Reddy**, Manthan International School.

British Library Cataloguing-in-Publication Data
A catalogue record for this publication is available from the British Library.

Author: **Gurinder Chadha**
Expert reviewers: **Frank Akrofi** and **Samuel Yeboah**
Publisher: **Elaine Higgleton**
Product manager: **Jennifer Hall**
Copyeditor: **Mitch Fitton**
Proofreader: **Sarah Ryan**
Cover designer: **Gordon MacGilp**
Cover artwork: **Maria Herbert-Liew**
Internal designer and illustrator: **PDQ Media**
Typesetter: **PDQ Media**
Production controllers: **Sarah Hovell and Lyndsey Rogers**
Printed in India by Multivista Global Pvt. Ltd.

This book is produced from independently certified FSC™ paper to ensure responsible forest management. For more information visit: www.harpercollins.co.uk/green

Cambridge International Education material in this publication is reproduced under licence and remains the intellectual property of Cambridge University Press & Assessment.

This text has not been through the endorsement process for the Cambridge Pathway. Any references or materials related to answers, grades, papers or examinations are based on the opinion of the author(s). The Cambridge International Education syllabus or curriculum framework associated assessment guidance material and specimen papers should always be referred to for definitive guidance.

The publishers gratefully acknowledge the permission granted to reproduce the copyright material in this book. Every effort has been made to trace copyright holders and to obtain their permission for the use of copyright material. The publishers will gladly receive any information enabling them to rectify any error or omission at the first opportunity.

Photographs
P 81 Shutterstock/Triff; p 116 Shutterstock/Grigvovan; p 142 Shutterstock/Urbanbuzz; p 150 Shutterstock/Arvitalyaart

Contents

Contents

Answers for all the questions in this Workbook are available from
http://www.collins.co.uk/internationalresources.

Making measurements

Student's Book pages 10–13 | Syllabus learning objectives 1.1.1–1.1.3

1 For each question, circle the correct answer.

a How many cm are there in 1 m? [1]

A 0.01 **B** 0.1 **C** 100 **D** 10 000

b How many cm^3 are there in 1 m^3? [1]

A 10 **B** 100 **C** 1000 **D** 1 000 000

2 A student measures the length of a magnet using a plastic ruler. The ruler is placed slightly away from the edge of the magnet and the student measures the length of the magnet from the position shown in the diagram.

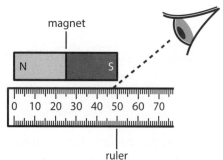

The student records the length of the magnet as 48 mm.

Explain why this measurement is incorrect and suggest the correct length of the magnet.

....

.... [2]

3 The diagram shows some water in a measuring cylinder.

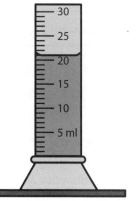

a What is the volume of the water?
Give a reason for your answer.

....

.... [2]

b A small solid metal cube is gently dropped into the water. It sinks to the bottom of the measuring cylinder. The new volume reading taken from the measuring cylinder is 29 ml, where 1 ml $= 1$ cm^3.

Determine the volume of the metal cube in cm^3.

volume = ... cm^3 [1]

c Each side of the metal cube has length 2.0 cm.

i Calculate the volume of the metal cube.

volume = ... cm^3 [2]

ii State how your value in **(c)(i)** compares with the value in **(b)**.

.... [1]

4 **a** In an experiment, a small metal ball is dropped from a great height into a tray of soft sand. The diameter D of the crater formed by the impact of the ball with the sand is measured to the nearest mm using a ruler.

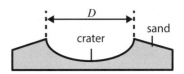

The experiment is repeated five times. The results are shown below.

Diameter D / mm	12	10	19	11	12

i Identify the most likely incorrect reading of the diameter.

.... [1]

ii Determine the average diameter of the crater without the value identified in your answer above. Write your answer to the nearest mm.

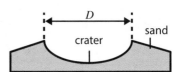

average diameter .... mm [2]

b The table below shows some results collected by a student investigating how the length *L* of a pendulum affects the time it takes to make 20 oscillations (or swings).

Length *L* / cm	Time for 20 oscillations / s	Period / s
30.0	22.0	
60.0	31.1	

A stopwatch is used to time the 20 oscillations. The time for one complete oscillation is called the *period*.

i Complete the last column in the table. Write your answer to one decimal place. [2]

ii Use the table to suggest how the length affects the period.

.... [1]

iii Explain why it is sensible to determine the period by timing 20 oscillations rather than the timing a single oscillation.

....

.... [2]

• •

Scalars and vectors

Student's Book pages 13–15 | Syllabus learning objectives
SUPPLEMENT 1.1.4–1.1.7

• •

1 Complete the two sentences below.

SUPPLEMENT

- A .... quantity only has magnitude. [1]

- A vector quantity has both magnitude and .... [1]

2

SUPPLEMENT

A list of scalar and vector quantities is given in the table below.

Correctly identify each quantity by placing a tick ✓ in the appropriate column. The first two quantities have already been identified for you.

Quantity	Scalar	Vector
Acceleration		✓
Distance	✓	
Electric field strength		
Energy		
Force		
Gravitational field strength		
Mass		
Momentum		
Speed		
Temperature		
Time		
Velocity		
Weight		

[11]

3

SUPPLEMENT

This question is about adding some vector quantities. In each case, determine the magnitude (**size**) and direction of the resultant vector.

a

magnitude of force = ... N

direction of force: .... [2]

b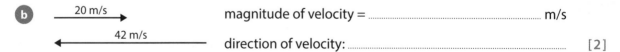

magnitude of velocity = ... m/s

direction of velocity: .... [2]

c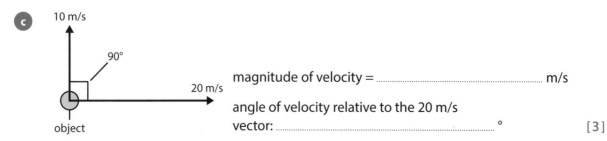

magnitude of velocity = ... m/s

angle of velocity relative to the 20 m/s vector: .... ° [3]

d

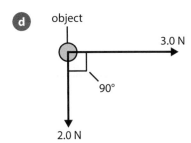

object

3.0 N

90°

2.0 N

magnitude of force = ... N

angle of force relative to the 3.0 N vector: .... ° [3]

4 Determine the magnitude and direction of the resultant of the two forces shown in
SUPPLEMENT **3(d)** by doing a scale drawing (graphical method).

> **TIP**
>
> You can use 2.0 cm to represent
> 1.0 N for your scale drawing.

magnitude of force = ... N

angle of force relative to the 3.0 N vector: .... ° [4]

• •

Speed and velocity

Student's Book pages 18–20 | Syllabus learning objectives 1.2.1–1.2.3

....

1 **a** Complete each equation by giving the name of the missing quantity.

i speed = distance ÷ .... [1]

ii distance = ... × time [1]

b A student wants to determine the average speed of a trolley rolling down a ramp from point A to point B.

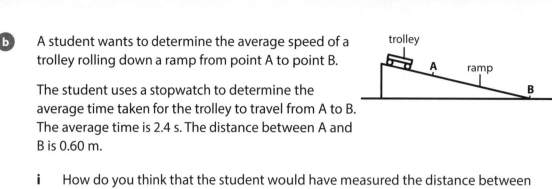

The student uses a stopwatch to determine the average time taken for the trolley to travel from A to B. The average time is 2.4 s. The distance between A and B is 0.60 m.

i How do you think that the student would have measured the distance between A and B?

.... [1]

ii Calculate the average speed of the trolley.

average speed = ... m/s [2]

2 **a** The table below shows the time taken by three cars A, B and C to travel a distance of 2.0 km.

Car	A	B	C
Time / minutes	3.0	3.4	2.7

i Which car is the fastest? Explain your answer.

....

.... [2]

ii Use the table to determine the average speed of car A in m/s.

TIP
For the speed to be in m/s you need to first convert the distance from km to m. The kilo (k) prefix is equal to 1000 or 10^3. The time also needs to be converted in seconds. There are 60 s in one minute.

average speed = ... m/s [3]

b The speed of a motorboat is 34 m/s.

i Calculate the distance travelled by the motorboat in a time of 20 s.

distance = ... m   [2]

ii Calculate the time taken by motorboat to travel 10 m. Write your answer to two significant figures.

time = ... s   [2]

3 ▶ **a** A ball falling vertically hits the floor with a velocity +4.0 m/s. The ball bounces back up at the same speed.

What is the velocity of ball immediately after impact with the floor? Circle your answer.

A +4.0 m/s   B +8.0 m/s   C −4.0 m/s   D 0 m/s   [1]

b Describe the difference between speed and velocity.

....

....   [2]

Distance–time graphs

Student's Book pages 21–22 | Syllabus learning objectives 1.2.4–1.2.6

1 ▶ Three distance–time graphs for an object are shown below. For each distance–time graph, describe the motion of the object and give a reason for your answer.

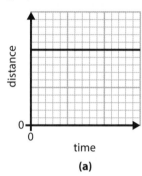
(a)

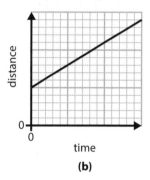
(b)

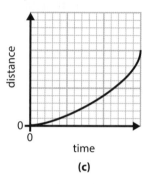
(c)

a ....

.... [2]

b ....

.... [2]

c ....

.... [2]

2 ▶ The distance–time graph for a walker is shown below.

a By examining the time intervals 0 s to 10 s and 10 s to 20 s, state when the walker is travelling the slowest.

TIP
The command term 'state' requires a brief answer with no reasoning.

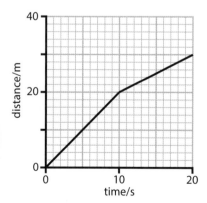

.... [1]

b   Calculate the speed of the walker at time $t = 5.0$ s.

speed = ... m/s   [2]

c   How does the gradient of the line at time $t = 5.0$ s relate to your answer in **(b)**?

.... [1]

3   The distance–time graph for a car is shown below.

a   Determine the total distance travelled by the car in 20 s.

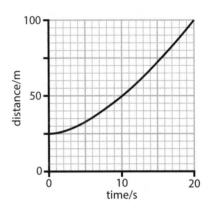

total distance = ... m   [1]

b   Determine the constant speed v of the car after 10 s.

v = ... m/s

Acceleration

Student's Book pages 22–27 | Syllabus learning objectives 1.2.7–1.2.8;
SUPPLEMENT 1.2.9–1.2.13

....

1 ▶ **a** What is the approximate acceleration of free fall of an object falling near the
surface of the Earth? Circle your answer.

A 9.8 m/s **B** 9.8 m/s^2 **C** 10 m/s **D** 10 N [1]

b **i** On the axes opposite, sketch the speed–time graph
for an object released from rest and falling vertically
downwards near the surface of the Earth.

Assume air resistance is negligible.

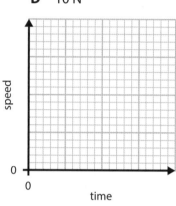

[2]

ii How would the speed–time graph above change when the object has an initial
downward velocity at the start? Explain your answer.

....

....
[2]

SUPPLEMENT **iii** Briefly describe how the speed–time graph above would change if air resistance
was **not** ignored.

....
[1]

2 ▶ The speed–time graph for a cyclist is
shown below.

a Describe the motion of the cyclist.

....

....

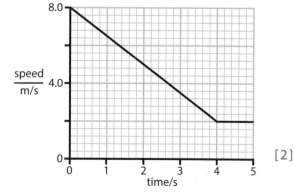

[2]

b Calculate the total distance travelled by the cyclist from time $t = 0$ to time $t = 5.0$ s.

total distance =... m   [4]

SUPPLEMENT

c Use the graph to calculate the magnitude of the deceleration of the cyclist at time $t = 2.5$ s.

TIP
Deceleration is negative acceleration, which implies that the velocity decreases with time.

magnitude of deceleration =.. m/s^2 [3]

3 A test rocket is fired upwards. It lifts up vertically and after a short period of time it falls
SUPPLEMENT freely under gravity back towards the surface of the Earth. Well before impacting the
Earth's surface, the rocket had reached its *terminal velocity*.

a During one stage in its initial upward motion, the speed of the rocket changes from
100 m/s to 190 m/s in a time period of 3.6 s. Calculate the acceleration of the rocket.

acceleration =..m/s^2 [3]

b Name the **two** forces acting on the rocket as it falls towards the Earth at its
terminal velocity.

1 ....   **2** ....   [2]

c State what happens to the velocity and acceleration of the rocket as it falls towards the Earth at its terminal velocity.

....

.... **[2]**

• •

Mass and weight

Student's Book pages 33–36 | Syllabus learning objectives 1.3.1–1.3.4; SUPPLEMENT 1.3.5

....

1 **a** What instrument can you use in the laboratory to compare weights (and masses)? Circle your answer.

A balance   **B** measuring cylinder   **C** metre rule   **D** stopwatch   **[1]**

b Which statement below is correct for defining the mass of an object? Circle your answer.

A Mass is a measure of how many atoms there are in an object relative to the observer.

B Mass is a measure of the kilograms of an object relative to the observer.

C Mass is a measure of the quantity of matter in an object at rest relative to the observer.

D Mass is a measure of the weight of an object relative to the observer.   **[1]**

SUPPLEMENT

c Complete the sentence below.

The weight of an object is the effect of a .... field on

a ....   **[1]**

2 **a** In words, define gravitational field strength g.

.... **[1]**

b State what gravitational field strength is equivalent to for an object falling towards the surface of the Earth (or another planet).

.... [1]

c Write an equation for gravitational field strength g in terms of gravitational force (or its weight) F acting on an object and its mass m.

.... [1]

d The gravitational field strength close to the surface of the Earth is 9.8 N/kg. Complete the table below, where m is the mass of the object and F is the gravitational force acting on the object at the Earth's surface. Write your values to two significant figures.

m / kg	F / N
45	
	1200
0.20	

[3]

3 Scientists used a space probe to determine the tiny force experienced by a small metal ball on a certain planet. The mass of the metal ball is 1.20 g and it experiences a gravitational force of 0.030 N.

a Calculate the gravitational field strength g.

$g =$... N/kg   [3]

b Suggest whether or not the space probe was on the surface of the Earth.

.... [1]

Density

Student's Book pages 39–42 | Syllabus learning objectives 1.4.1

....

1 ▶ **a**   Write an equation for density ρ of a material. Define any additional terms used.

....

.... [2]

b   The density of water is 1.0 g/cm^3.

What is the mass of the water with the following volumes?

i   volume $= 2.0$ cm^3 mass = ... g   [1]

ii   volume $= 10$ cm^3 mass = ... g   [1]

iii   volume $= 1000$ cm^3 mass = ... g   [1]

c   The density of a metal is 2.7 g/cm^3.

Calculate the density of the metal in kg/m^3.

TIP
There are 1000 g in 1 kg and there are 1 000 000 cm^3 in 1 m^3 or 1 cm $= 10^{-6}$ m^3

density = ... kg/m^3 [3]

2 ▶ **a**   Calculate the volume of a material given its density is 8.0 g/cm^3 and it has mass of 96 g.

volume = ...cm^3 [3]

b   The density of a rock is 550 kg/m^3 and it has a volume of 0.020 m^3. Calculate the mass of the rock in kg.

mass = ... kg   [3]

c A column of liquid has cross-sectional area 3.2 cm^2 and height 15 cm. The mass of the liquid column is 36 g. Calculate the density of the liquid in g/cm^3.

density = ...g/cm^3 [3]

3 The table below shows the density of three metals.

A student has a rectangular block of metal. The length of the block is 4.0 cm, its width is 2.0 cm and its height is 2.5 cm. The mass of the block is 156 g.

Metal	Aluminium	Steel	Gold
Density (g/cm^3)	2.7	7.8	19.3

a Calculate the volume of the metal block.

volume = ...cm^3 [1]

b Determine the density of the metal and use the table above to identify the metal.

density = ...g/cm^3 [2]

The metal is .... [1]

Determining density

Student's Book pages 42–45 | Syllabus learning objectives 1.4.2–1.4.3; SUPPLEMENT 1.4.4

....

1 Describe how you can determine the density of a wooden block in the shape of a cube. In your description, include:

- the equipment you would use

- the measurements you need to take

- how the data collected will be used to determine the density.

....

....

....

....

....

[4]

2 The information opposite is collected by a student who is determining the density of vegetable oil.

Mass of empty measuring cylinder	120 g
Volume of oil in measuring cylinder	42 cm^3
Total mass of measuring cylinder with the oil	156 g

Use the information provided to calculate the density of the oil.

density = ...g/cm^3 [3]

3 A student is given a measuring cylinder and a supply of water. A digital balance is also available.

Describe how the student can determine the density of the metal bolt shown below. In your description, include:

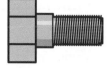

- the measurements you need to take

- how the data collected will be used to determine the density.

....

....

....

....

....

....

....

.... **[4]**

4 **a** The density of wax is about 0.9 g/cm^3 and the density of water is 1.0 g/cm^3.

Explain whether or not the wax will float or sink in water.

....

.... **[2]**

b The table below shows the density of three liquids.

Liquid	Oil	Water	Honey
Density $\left(\text{g/cm}^3\right)$	0.92	1.00	1.45

When liquid X is gently poured onto oil or water it sinks but it floats on honey.

Which condition below best describes the density of liquid X? Circle your answer.

A less than 0.92 g/cm^3 **B** less than 1.00 g/cm^3

C between 1.00 g/cm^3 to 1.45 g/cm^3 **D** more than 1.45 g/cm^3 **[1]**

Forces

Student's Book pages 45–54 | Syllabus learning objectives 1.5.1.1; 1.5.1.3–1.5.1.8

1 Various forces act on an object. Tick ✓ all the effects that these forces can have on the object.

Forces can change the object's …	Place a tick ✓ here if correct
colour	
shape	
size	
direction of travel	
speed	
weight	

[1]

2 A heavy box is pushed along a level ground at a constant speed. The force pushing the box to the right is 60 N.

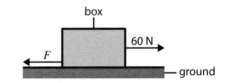

a Describe what is meant by solid friction in relation to the box.

.... [1]

b State the value of the frictional force F acting on the box.

$F = $ .... N [1]

c What is the resultant force acting on the box? Give a reason for your answer.

TIP
A non-zero resultant force is needed to change the velocity of an object, either by changing its direction or its speed

....

.... [2]

3 In the two examples below, each object is **falling** vertically downwards at a *constant* speed.

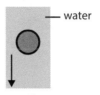

— water

a Parachutist falling through air

b Ball falling in water

TIP
Drag refers to the frictional force acting on an object moving through a liquid or a gas

In each case, show the directions of the weight and the drag. [2]

4 In each case below determine the magnitude, and direction if any, of the resultant force and state whether or not its velocity will change.

a ....

10 N ← ☐ → 10 N

.... [2]

b ....

5 N ↑

12 N ↓

.... [2]

c ....

0.5 N ← ☐ → 1.7 N

← 1.1 N

.... [2]

Springs

Student's Book pages 54–58 | Syllabus learning objectives 1.5.1.2;
SUPPLEMENT 1.5.1.9–1.5.1.10

1 A rubber band can be extended as shown in the diagram.

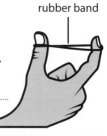

rubber band

Describe how you can determine the extension of the rubber band as shown.

....

.... [2]

2 The load–extension graph for an elastic metal wire is shown opposite.

a Explain how the extension of the wire is affected by the applied load (**force**).

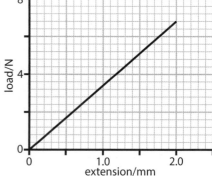

....

....

.... [2]

b On the same axes, sketch a graph for a metal wire that is much 'stiffer' than the wire shown in **(a)**. [1]

3 **a** Which quantity is defined as '*force per unit extension*'? Circle your answer.

SUPPLEMENT

A acceleration   **C** force constant

B density   **D** speed   [1]

b A force of 12 N extends a spring by 20 cm. Calculate the force constant of the spring in N/m.

force constant=.. N/m [3]

4

A student is investigating the behaviour of a spring. The data points are plotted on the axes shown below.

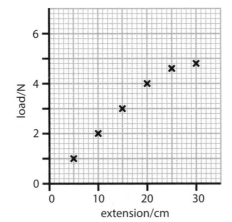

a Draw a suitable line through the data points. [1]

b Calculate the force constant of the spring using load = 3.0 N.

force constant = ... N/cm [2]

c Determine the gradient of the straight-line section of the graph.

State how it compares with your answer in **(b)**.

gradient = ...

.... [2]

d On the graph, identify the limit of proportionality of the spring. [1]

SUPPLEMENT Understanding the equation $F = ma$

Student's Book pages 59–60 | Syllabus learning objective
SUPPLEMENT 1.5.1.11

1 A very useful equation in physics is $F = ma$.

SUPPLEMENT

a Identify all the terms in this equation.

F: .... m: .... a: .... [1]

b Complete the following two equations showing the relationship between the quantities identified in **(a)**.

$a =$ .... $m =$ .... [1]

c Which of the following is the correct alternative unit for the newton (N)? Circle your answer.

A kg **B** m/s^2 **C** kg m s^2 **D** kg m/s^2 [1]

d The resultant force acting on a car is doubled. What happens to its acceleration? Give a reason for your answer.

....

.... [2]

e The direction of acceleration of an object is to the right. What is the direction of the resultant force?

....

.... [1]

2 The diagram below shows the horizontal forces acting on a 900 kg mass car when it is
SUPPLEMENT about to move off **(a)**, and then a short time later **(b)**.

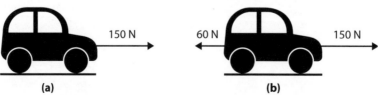

(a)   (b)

Calculate the acceleration of the car in each case.

(a)   acceleration = ... m/s^2 [2]

> **TIP**
>
> In the equation $F = ma$, F is the **total** or **resultant** force

(b)   acceleration = ... m/s^2 [3]

3   The diagram opposite shows an air-powered toy rocket. The rocket lifts off vertically when the someone pushes on the foot pump.

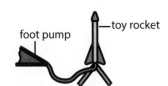

The mass of the rocket is 0.050 kg. The vertical upwards force on the rocket during lift-off is 0.70 N.

(a)   Show that the resultant force on the rocket at lift-off is 0.21 N.

[2]

(b)   Calculate the acceleration of the rocket at lift-off.

                                      acceleration = ... m/s^2 [2]

Circular motion

Student's Book pages 60–62 | Syllabus learning objective
SUPPLEMENT 1.5.1.12

1

The diagram opposite shows the view from above of a car moving in a clockwise direction in a circular path. The speed of the car is constant.

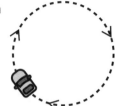

a Explain what happens to the velocity of the car as it moves in this circular path.

[2]

b On the diagram, draw an arrow to show the direction of the velocity of the car. [1]

c What are the relative directions of the velocity of the car and the force responsible for the circular motion of the car?

[1]

2

SUPPLEMENT

Complete the table by naming the force that provides the centripetal force for the circular motion of the object.

Object	Name of force providing the centripetal force
Moon orbiting a planet.	
Stone tied to a string that is swung horizontally in a circular path.	
Car going around a roundabout.	

[3]

3

SUPPLEMENT

a The diagram opposite shows an athlete swinging a metal ball in a horizontal circle of constant radius.

What happens to the force acting on the metal ball as its speed increases?

[1]

b Complete the two sentences below.

• At a constant speed, and for a given mass, the force perpendicular to circular motion

increases as the radius of the circular path .... [1]

• For a given speed and radius, the force perpendicular to circular motion ....

as the mass of the object is increased. [1]

Moments and centre-of-gravity

Student's Book pages 62–67 | Syllabus learning objectives 1.5.2.1–1.5.2.4;
SUPPLEMENT 1.5.2.6 ; 1.5.3.1–1.5.3.3

1 Which of the following is **not** an example of a turning effect? Circle your answer.

A A rocket flying in a straight-line in space.

B Lifting a wheelbarrow.

C Opening a door.

D Two children going up and down on a seesaw. [1]

2 The diagram opposite shows a wheelbarrow lifted and in equilibrium. The weight of the wheelbarrow and its contents is 400 N. The line of action of the weight is at a perpendicular distance of 0.35 m from the bottom of the wheel (**pivot**) B.

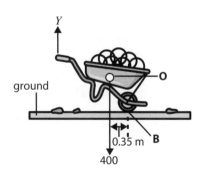

The point O is the centre of gravity of the wheelbarrow and its contents.

a State what is meant by centre of gravity of an object.

.... [1]

b State which force (Y or 400 N) creates a clockwise moment about point B and which creates an anticlockwise moment about point B.

clockwise moment: .... anticlockwise moment: .... [1]

c State the resultant force and resultant moment on the wheelbarrow.

.... [2]

d Calculate the moment of the weight about point B.

moment = ... N m [2]

e Without any further calculations, state the moment of the force Y about point B.

.... [1]

3 Two beams are in equilibrium.

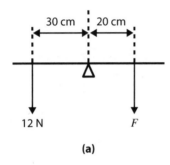

(a)

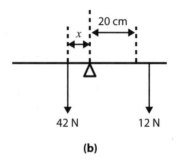

(b)

For beam **(a)**, determine the force F.

$F = $ .... N [3]

For beam **(b)**, determine the distance x.

$x = $ .... cm [3]

4 A student is investigating the principle of moments. The diagram opposite shows a ruler pivoted at its middle with three loads hanging from it. The ruler is horizontal and in equilibrium.

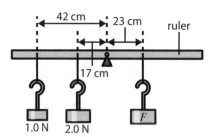

a State the resultant moment about the pivot.

.... [1]

b Detemine the force F exerted by the load on the right. Write your answer to two significant figures.

$F =$ .... N [4]

5 A student is determining the centre of gravity of a flat irregular metal plate.

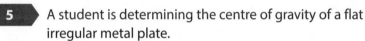

The diagram opposite shows a flat irregular metal plate. It is hung vertically from each of three holes in turn and each time, a vertical line is drawn on the plate.

a State one precaution you would take in ensuring that the centre of gravity lies along the vertical line drawn.

.... [1]

b On the diagram, indicate the position of the centre of gravity of the metal plate with a letter O. [1]

6 This question is about stability of a bottle that is tilted in the vertical plane.

The diagram shows the bottle in three different positions. The centre of gravity of the bottle in each case is shown by the spot ● in the middle. The vertical force at the pivoting point of the bottle is shown in each case.

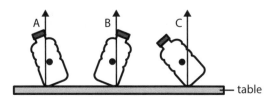

a Draw an arrow to show the weight of the bottle in each case. [1]

b Explain in which of the three positions shown, the bottle is unstable and will topple over.

....

.... [2]

• •

Momentum

Student's Book pages 72–77 | Syllabus learning objectives
SUPPLEMENT 1.6.1–1.6.4

• •

1 **a** Define momentum of an object.

SUPPLEMENT

.... [1]

b Calculate the magnitude of the momentum of an athlete of mass 60 kg running at a speed of 5.0 m/s to the *left*.

momentum = ... kg m/s [2]

c What is the momentum of the same athlete running at the same speed to the *right*?

.... [1]

2 A footballer kicks a stationary ball.

SUPPLEMENT The diagram below shows the momentum of the footballer's foot (and leg) just before the ball is kicked and the momentum of the foot and ball immediately after being kicked.

before   after

The mass of the ball is 0.45 kg.

a Calculate the momentum p of the foot (and leg) after the ball has been kicked.

Explain your answer.

....

$p =$ .... kg m/s [3]

b Show that the speed of the ball immediately after being kicked is 20 m/s. [2]

c The foot is in contact with the ball for 0.12 s.

Calculate the force exerted on the ball by the foot.

force = ... N [3]

3 **a** Complete the equation: impulse = force ×... [1]

SUPPLEMENT

b The momentum of a speeding car changes from 5000 kg m/s to 7000 kg m/s.

What is the impulse of the force acting on the car? Give reason for your answer.

....

.... [2]

4 A student is investigating collisions of laboratory trolleys.

SUPPLEMENT

In one experiment, a trolley travelling at 2.0 m/s crashes head-on into an identical trolley that was initially at rest. The trolleys join together and move as one.

Explain the common speed of the two trolleys immediately after the crash.

....

....

.... [3]

Energy

Student's Book pages 81–87 | Syllabus learning objectives 1.7.1.1–1.7.1.3;
SUPPLEMENT 1.7.1.4–1.7.1.6

1 Energy can be stored – the energy stores have different names. For example, when a rubber band is extended the energy stored within the rubber band is called elastic potential energy.

Complete the table below, by identifying the energy store for each description.

Description	Name of energy store(s)
Energy in cooking oil.	
Energy of hot water to make tea or coffee.	
Energy in the food we eat.	
Energy in the nuclei of radioactive atoms.	
Energy of a space probe moving between two planets.	
Energy stored between an electron and a nucleus.	

[7]

2 A high-speed train suddenly brakes and comes to a halt after travelling a short distance along the track. The wheels of the train skid along the track. Noise is generated as the train slows down. The wheels of the train and the track get very hot.

a Identify the final energy store in this process.

kinetic energy ⟶ .... energy   [1]

b Mechanical work is done by friction to slow down the train.

What is also produced in this process as energy is transferred between the energy stores identified in **(a)**? Circle your answer.

A electrical   **B** light   **C** nuclear   **D** sound   [1]

SUPPLEMENT

c Complete the Sankey diagram for the train coming to a halt.

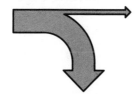

[2]

3 A block of wood of 0.80 kg is placed on a ramp
SUPPLEMENT and released from rest from point A. It slides
down the ramp picking up speed. At the bottom
B of the ramp, the block has speed 2.0 m/s.

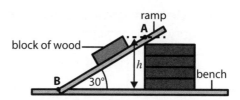

The distance between A and B is 1.5 m. The ramp makes
an angle of 30° to the horizontal.

a Show that the initial height h of the block is 0.75 m.

[2]

b Calculate the change in gravitational potential energy ΔE_p of the block as it slides from
A to B.

$\Delta E_p =$.. J   [3]

c Calculate the kinetic energy E_k of the block at the bottom of the ramp.

$E_k =$.. J   [3]

d Use the principle of conservation of energy to explain why the two values in **(b)** and **(c)**
are not the same.

....

.... [2]

Energy resources

Student's Book pages 87–94 | Syllabus learning objectives 1.7.3.1–1.7.3.3;
SUPPLEMENT 1.7.3.4–1.7.3.7

1 **a** Biofuels, fossil fuels and nuclear fuels are used in the production of electricity in power stations. In these power stations in the first stage, water is heated in a boiler using energy from one of these fuels.

Complete the diagram below by identifying the last two stages in the production of electricity from the power station.

[2]

b Complete the sentences below.

.... energy resource, when used, will be naturally replenished

over time. An example of this type of energy resource is .... [2]

c A non-renewable energy resource will be gone forever once used.

Tick ✓ all the non-renewable energy resources in the list below.

- biofuels

- electromagnetic waves from
  the Sun

- fossil fuels

- geothermal resources

- nuclear fuels

[1]

2 The diagram opposite shows a tidal power station at the mouth of a river meeting the sea **(estuary)**. The turbine blades rotate and the generator produces electrical power when the tide comes in or when the tide goes out. The power station helps with the transmission of electrical power across the land.

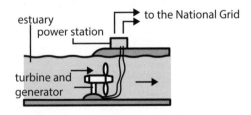

a Suggest **one** environmental disadvantage of power generated using this tidal system.

.... [1]

b Other than cost, state **two** advantages of using the tidal system for generating electrical power rather than an oil-fired power station.

....

.... [2]

3 **a** Complete the last column of the table below.

Energy resource	Energy store
Biofuel	
Fossil fuel (coal, gas and oil)	
Geothermal	
Hydroelectricity	
Nuclear fuel	
Solar	
Tidal	
Water waves	
Wind	

[9]

b In a certain household, water is heated using an electric heater. The water is subsequently stored in a large metal storage tank until it is required.

If the water is not used for some hours, it will eventually cool down because of transfer of its internal (thermal) energy to the surroundings, and the electric heater must be switched on again.

Suggest **one** way in which the householder can reduce the energy wasted in this way.

.... [1]

4 **a** Complete the sentence below:

The radiation from the Sun is the main source of energy for all our energy resources

except for g.., n..

and t.. . [3]

b The race is on to produce large scale electricity using nuclear fusion. Very high temperatures are required to trigger nuclear fusion between hydrogen nuclei to produce helium nuclei. Some scientists think that this may happen by about 2040.

i Suggest why energy from nuclear fusion would be preferable to energy produced from burning fossil fuels.

.... [1]

ii Name the hot glowing ball of gas that releases energy naturally from nuclear fusion.

.... [1]

c At present, some electricity is produced by nuclear fission power stations. The efficiency of a typical power station producing electricity is about 35%.

A nuclear power station produces a power output of 1.2 GW. Calculate the total power input. Give your answer in GW, where 1 GW= 10^9 W.

total power input =.. GW [3]

d A geothermal power station produces 30 000 J in a particular time. The total energy input to the power station in the same period of time is 375 000 J. Calculate the efficiency of this type of power station.

efficiency =..% [3]

Work done and power

Student's Book pages 94–100 | Syllabus learning objectives 1.7.2.1–1.7.2.2; 1.7.4.1

....

1 A vase is lifted from the floor onto a shelf. Which two quantities are required to calculate the work done on the vase? Circle your answer.

A The mass of the vase and its volume.

B The mass of the vase and the time taken to lift the vase.

C The weight of the vase and the height of the shelf from the floor.

D The weight of the vase and the time taken to lift the vase.   [1]

2 **a** Complete the sentence below.

The mechanical or electrical work done on an object is equal to the ....

transferred.   [1]

b The unit of work done is the joule (**J**). Which of the following is correct? Circle your answer.

A $1\,J = 1\,N\,m$ **C** $1\,J = 1\,N/m$

B $1\,J = 1\,kg\,m$ **D** $1\,J = 1\,kg\,m/s^2$ [1]

c The force acting on an object is F and the distance moved by the object in the direction of the force is d. Complete the missing items in the table below.

$F/\,N$	$d/\,m$	Work done / J	Energy transferred / J
100	50		
	160	8000	
45		270	

[6]

3 **a** Define power in terms of work done.

.... [1]

b The unit of power is the watt (W). Which of the following is correct? Circle your answer.

A 1 W = 1 J s   **C** 1 W = 1 N s

B 1 W = 1 J/s   **D** 1 W = 1 N/s   [1]

c A car is travelling on a straight road. The driver applies the brakes. The kinetic energy of the car changes from 200 kJ to 50 kJ in 7.5 s.

i Calculate the braking power of the car.

power =.. W   [3]

ii What energy store is the kinetic energy of the car transferred to?

.... [1]

4 The output power of a water pump is 200 W.

a What is the energy transferred per second by the water pump?

.... [1]

b Calculate the energy transferred by the water pump in a time of 30 minutes.

TIP
You must convert the time into seconds. There are 60 s in one minute.

energy transferred =.. J   [2]

5 The falling water from a dam is used to generate electrical power.

In a time of 1.0 minutes (60 s), the mass of water falling through a height of 20 m onto the turbine blades of the generator at the bottom of the fall is 30 000 kg.

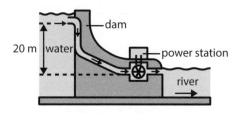

a Show that the weight of 30 000 kg of water is 294 000 N. [1]

b Calculate the work done by the force of gravity on the 30 000 kg mass of water falling through 20 m.

work done =.. J [2]

c Calculate the total power input to the generator.

total power input =.. W [2]

Pressure

Student's Book pages 106–108 | Syllabus learning objectives 1.8.1–1.8.2

1 **a** Write an equation for pressure p in terms of the force F and the area A.

.... [1]

b In an experiment, a student has the force acting on a surface in newtons (N) and the area over which the force acts in cm^2.

The pressure is calculated as 1.5 N/cm^2. What is this pressure in N/m^2?

TIP
There are 100 cm in 1 m, therefore 10^4 cm^2 in 1 m^2.

pressure =.. N/m^2 [2]

c All the objects below are drawn to scale, and each object has the **same** weight.

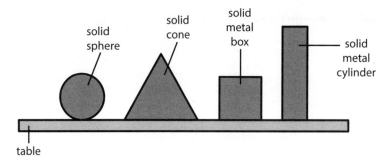

Explain which object exerts the least pressure on the table.

....

.... [2]

d Explain why is easier to cut bread, or fruit, with a sharp knife rather than a blunt knife.

....

.... [2]

2 The weight of a person is 520 N when they are standing on soft sand. The **total** surface area of the shoes the person is wearing is 140 cm^2.

a Calculate the pressure p exerted by the person on the soft sand.

$p =$.. N/cm^2 [2]

b Without any further calculation, explain the effect on the pressure exerted when the person stands on just one leg.

....

.... [2]

3 ▶ A concrete column in the shape of a long cylinder is resting on the ground as shown. The cross-sectional area of the concrete column is 0.52 m², and its mass is 9.0 tonnes. (1 tonne = 1000 kg).

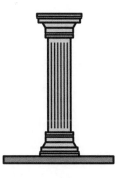

Calculate the pressure, in N/m², exerted by the concrete column on the ground.

pressure = ...N/m² [3]

Pressure in fluids

Student's Book pages 108–112 | Syllabus learning objectives 1.8.3; SUPPLEMENT 1.8.4

1 ▶ **a** The diagram shows a polystyrene sphere being pushed into water. Describe how the pressure exerted by the water on the sphere changes as the sphere is pushed deeper into the water.

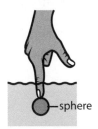

sphere

....

....

[1]

b Three identical measuring cylinders are filled with liquids of different densities. The level of the liquid in each cylinder is the same.

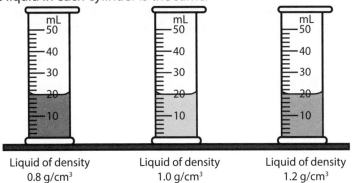

Liquid of density 0.8 g/cm³   Liquid of density 1.0 g/cm³   Liquid of density 1.2 g/cm³

Which liquid exerts the least pressure at the base of the cylinder? Give a reason for your answer.

....

.... [2]

2 **a** The density of seawater is about 1000 kg/m^3. A diver descends into seawater to a depth of 6.2 m. Calculate the change in the pressure Δp.

SUPPLEMENT

TIP
1 pascal (Pa) = 1 N/m^2

$\Delta p =$.. Pa [3]

b The barreleye is a fish that lives at a depth of 1.0 km in seawater. The pressure at such depths is almost 100 times more than atmospheric pressure $(1.0 \times 10^5$ Pa).

i Calculate the change in pressure due to seawater at a depth of 1.0 km.

change in pressure =.. Pa [3]

ii The total pressure on the barreleye fish is equal to your answer in **(i)** plus atmospheric pressure (which acts on the surface of the seawater).

Is the sentence about the 'pressure being almost 100 times more than atmospheric pressure' correct? Support your answer with a calculation.

....

....

.... [2]

iii   On the axes below, sketch a graph of change in pressure against depth of seawater.
You are not expected to show any numerical values on the axes.

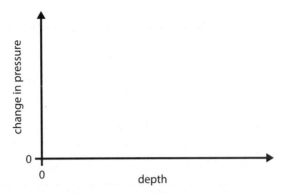

[2]

Matter and Brownian motion

Student's Book pages 127–132 | Syllabus learning objectives 2.1.1.1–2.1.1.2;
2.1.2.1–2.1.2.5; SUPPLEMENT 2.1.2.6–2.1.2.8

1 ▶ The table below has some descriptions that relate to the three states of matter – solid, liquid and gas. Complete the last column by identifying the state of matter. The first one has been done for you.

Description	State of matter
The particles (atoms) are arranged in a regular pattern and do not move apart from each other.	Solid
Particles move very fast with a range of speeds and directions.	
The substance will take the shape and volume of the container.	
A solid will change to this state of matter when its temperature is increased.	
The particles vibrate about fixed positions.	
A gas will change to this state of matter when its temperature is decreased.	

[5]

2 ▶ **a** Describe how the motion of the atoms of a gas is related to the temperature of the gas.

....

.... [2]

b Complete the sentences below.

• Gas atoms .... with the surface of a container produce pressure. [1]

- Gas atoms collide more frequently with the container walls when the temperature
  is ....   [1]

- At absolute zero, particles of matter have ....
  kinetic energy.   [1]

c Which statement is correct about the temperature of −273°C (absolute zero)? Circle
your answer.

A At this temperature particles have maximum kinetic energy.

B At this temperature the substance has zero volume.

C This is the lowest temperature possible.

D This is the temperature at which ice melts.   [1]

3

SUPPLEMENT

A container has a fixed amount of gas. Using the words below, explain how the gas
atoms exert pressure on the container walls.

force   change in momentum   collide   area

....

....

....

....

....   [4]

4 The diagram below shows an apparatus used to study Brownian motion of smoke particles suspended in air. Looking through the microscope, tiny specks of light are seen wriggling randomly in the field of view.

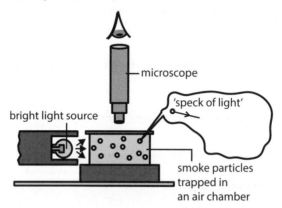

a According to a student, the specks of light are molecules of air. Give a reason why the student is incorrect.

.... [1]

b In the space provided next to the diagram, sketch the likely path of a single 'speck of light'. [2]

c Explain the path sketched in **(b)**.

....

.... [2]

SUPPLEMENT **d** Brownian motion of the smoke particles in air can be explained in terms of the random collisions of the smoke particles and what else? Circle your answer.

A fast-moving air molecules

B fast-moving smoke molecules

C slow-moving air molecules

D slow-moving smoke particles [1]

Gases

Student's Book pages 133–136 | Syllabus learning objectives 2.1.3.1–2.1.3.2;
SUPPLEMENT 2.1.3.3

....

1 This question is about temperature.

a Complete the word equation below.

temperature in kelvin (K) = temperature in degrees Celsius (°C) + ... [1]

b Complete the table below for the missing temperatures in either °C or K. One has already been done for you. [4]

Temperature in °C	200	150	0		
Temperature in K			273	173	73

c A student jokingly said that the temperature of an object found by astronomers in space was −500 °C. Explain what is wrong with this temperature.

....

.... [2]

2 A small metal container has a fixed amount of air. The temperature of the air inside is decreased.

a Suggest how you could decrease the temperature of the container in the laboratory.

.... [1]

b State whether the speed of the air particles decreases, increases or stays the same.

.... [1]

c State whether the pressure exerted by the air decreases, increases or stays the same.

.... [1]

3 A small rubber ball has some trapped air inside. The volume of the ball is decreased by pushing the ball against a wall.

Which statement below best describes why the pressure of the air inside the ball increases? Circle your answer. [1]

    A The air particles collide less frequently with each other.

    B The air particles collide with the inside of the ball more frequently.

    C The air particles move faster.

    D The air particles move further apart.

4 A helium-filled weather balloon is released from the surface of the Earth. The pressure exerted by the atmosphere on the balloon decreases as it climbs higher.

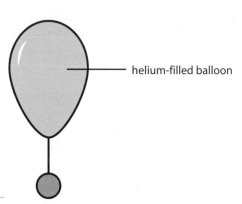

helium-filled balloon

a Explain what happens to the volume of the balloon as it climbs higher.

....

.... [2]

b The pressure inside the balloon is p and its volume is V. Complete the equation below:

$$p \times V = \text{..}$$ [1]

c The volume of the balloon at the surface of the Earth is 0.40 m^3 and the helium exerts a pressure of 1.0×10^5 Pa.

    i Calculate the volume of the balloon when the pressure drops to 0.10×10^5 Pa.

TIP
The volume is inversely proportional to the pressure. You can also use this idea to quickly solve the problem.

volume = ... m^3 [2]

ii Complete the graph below for the pressures 1.00×10^5 Pa to 0.25×10^5 Pa. One of the data points has already been plotted for you.

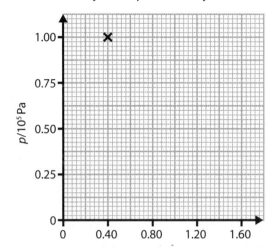

> **TIP**
>
> Start by plotting a few data points, and then draw a smooth curve with a sharp pencil.

[3]

5
SUPPLEMENT
A small amount of air is trapped in a glass tube. The pressure exerted by the air is p and it has volume V. The temperature of the surrounding air is kept constant. The table below shows some of the results collected in an experiment.

p / (N/cm^2)	1.00	1.30	1.73		
V / (cm^3)	52			26	20
$p \times V$ / (N cm)	52				

Complete the table. [4]

Thermal expansion

Student's Book pages 139–142 | Syllabus learning objectives 2.2.1.1–2.2.1.2;
SUPPLEMENT 2.2.1.3

1 **a** Circle the material that would expand the most, at constant pressure, for a given increase in temperature.

steel   water   brick   air   ice   [1]

b The table below has some statements related to thermal expansion. In the last column, state whether the statement is true or false.

Statement	True or false?
For a given increase in temperature, a liquid will expand much more than a gas.	
A metal bridge will be slightly longer during daytime than at night time.	
The volume of a gas, at a constant pressure, will increase when its temperature is increased.	
Increasing the temperature of a gas, at constant pressure, will increase the separation between the gas particles (atoms).	
All materials expand because the particles (atoms) that make them up become larger.	

[5]

2 **a** At room temperature, a steel rod cannot be slotted into a steel washer. The hole in the washer is slightly smaller than diameter of the steel rod. However, when the washer is heated to a very high temperature, the washer easily slips over the steel rod (which is at room temperature). Explain why this is so.

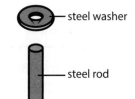
steel washer

steel rod

....

....

[2]

b All materials expand when heated. A long brick wall often has a gap. This gap is filled up with a flexible material. Describe what may happen to the wall if the gap was not there.

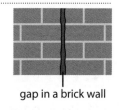
gap in a brick wall

....

....

[2]

3 ▶ **a** A block of copper is heated in an oven. Describe what happens to the motion and arrangement of the particles (atoms).

SUPPLEMENT

....

.... [2]

b This question is about two different metal strips (steel and brass) of similar width and length, joined together. This arrangement is known as a bimetallic strip.

brass

steel

For a given change in temperature, the volume of brass increases almost twice as much as steel.

Draw a diagram of the bimetallic strip when its temperature is increased. Explain the shape of the strip.

....

....

.... [3]

c A copper pipe has length 5.20 m at 20 °C. Its length increases by 0.0017% for every 1 °C increase in temperature.

Calculate the change in the length ΔL of the pipe when it has hot water at 90 °C flowing through it.

$\Delta L =$ .... m   [3]

4

SUPPLEMENT

For a given change in temperature, the volume of liquids increases by about four times more than solids. Circle the sentence below that represents the main reason for this. Circle your answer.

A The particles of liquids are separated more than the particles of solids.

B The particles of liquids are smaller than the particles of liquids.

C The particles of solids experience greater electrical forces than the particles of liquids.

D The particles of solids have greater speed than the particles of liquids. [1]

Specific heat capacity

Student's Book pages 142–145 | Syllabus learning objectives 2.2.2.1;
SUPPLEMENT 2.2.2.2–2.2.2.4

1 Internal energy of an object is defined as the total energy (kinetic and potential) of **all** the particles that make up the object.

a State how the internal energy of a liquid can be

i increased

.... [1]

ii decreased.

.... [1]

b Two copper blocks have the same temperature. One block has a mass of 200 g and the other has a mass of 800 g.

Which block has the greater internal energy? Give a reason for your answer.

200 g   800 g

....

.... [2]

2 **a**

Imagine that a student has a discussion about *temperature* and *internal energy* with you. The student thinks that both of these terms are the same.

How would you explain that the student is incorrect?

....

.... [2]

b Write an equation for the specific heat capacity c of a substance. Define any additional terms used.

[2]

c An experiment is being carried out to determine the specific heat capacity c of water. A small electrical heater is used to heat the water in a beaker. The power of the heater is known, so the increase in the thermal energy of the water can be determined.

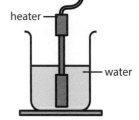

To determine c, what **other** measurements would you need and how would you take these measurements?

....

....

.... [3]

3 The table below shows the specific heat capacity c of some materials.

Material	Air	Copper	Olive oil	Steel	Water
c / J/kg °C	1000	390	1900	420	4200

55

a State which material of mass 0.10 kg will require the least amount of energy to change the temperature by 30 °C.

.... [1]

b Calculate the change energy supplied to 100 g of steel to change its temperature from 20 °C to 60 °C.

TIP
To have the change in energy in J you need to convert the mass into kg.

change in energy = ... J [3]

c A 2000 W heater is used to heat 0.50 kg of water for 60 s (1 minute).

i Show that the energy supplied to the water in 60 s is 120 000 J.

[1]

ii Calculate the increase in the temperature of the water.

increase in temperature = ... °C [3]

d The following data is collected in an experiment to determine the specific heat capacity of a material.

- energy supplied = 10 000 J
- mass of material = 200 g
- initial temperature = 10 °C
- final temperature = 36 °C

Determine the specific heat capacity c of the material, and identify it from the table given at the beginning of the question.

$c =$.. J/kg °C [2]

Material is: .... [1]

Melting, boiling and evaporation

Student's Book pages 145–147 | Syllabus learning objectives 2.2.3.1–2.2.3.5;
SUPPLEMENT 2.2.3.6–2.2.3.8

1 ▶ The table below shows some statements about the three processes of melting, boiling and evaporation. Place a tick in one of the last three columns to match the process with the correct statement.

Statement: In this process …	Melting	Boiling	Evaporation
cooling takes place.			
the more energetic particles escape the surface.			
there is a change of state without change in temperature.			
water changes state at 0 °C.			
water changes state at 100 °C.			

[4]

2 ▶ A small amount of solid wax in a beaker is heated using a Bunsen burner. The graph opposite shows the variation of temperature θ of the wax with time.

TIP
The wax is melting at 60 °C.

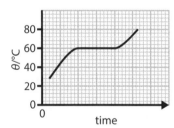

What is happening to the wax during the flat section of the graph? Circle your answer. [1]

    A   Energy from the Bunsen burner is used to change state to liquid wax.

    B   The internal energy of the wax stays the same.

    C   The temperature does not change because the wax stops absorbing energy.

    D   The beaker is taking all the energy from the wax.

3 **a** Condensation occurs when steam from water boiling in a kettle touches a cold metal spoon.

What is condensation and what happens to the particles of steam during this process?

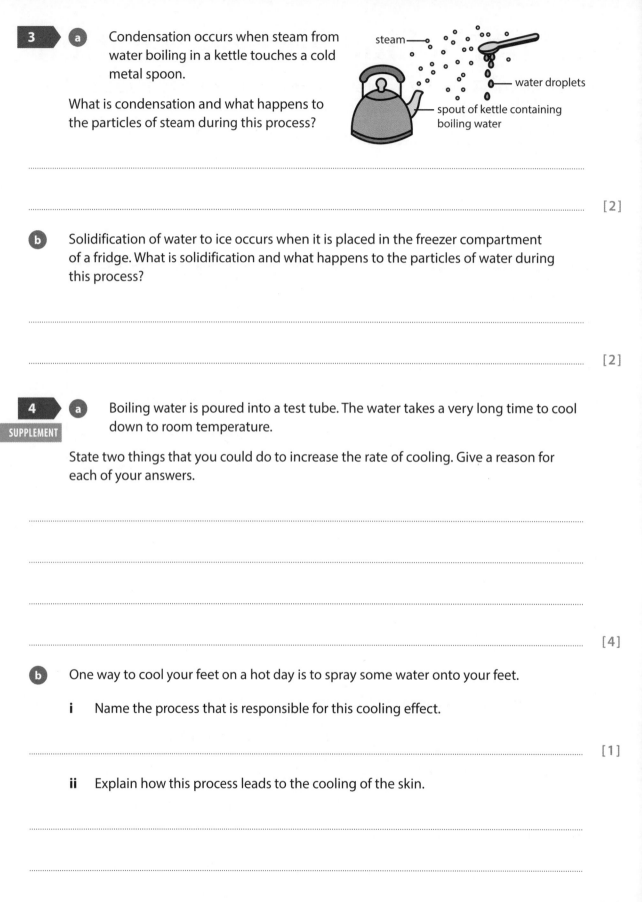

steam

water droplets

spout of kettle containing boiling water

....

....

[2]

b Solidification of water to ice occurs when it is placed in the freezer compartment of a fridge. What is solidification and what happens to the particles of water during this process?

....

....

[2]

4 **a** Boiling water is poured into a test tube. The water takes a very long time to cool down to room temperature.

SUPPLEMENT

State two things that you could do to increase the rate of cooling. Give a reason for each of your answers.

....

....

....

[4]

b One way to cool your feet on a hot day is to spray some water onto your feet.

i Name the process that is responsible for this cooling effect.

....

[1]

ii Explain how this process leads to the cooling of the skin.

....

....

....

58

[3]

c The table below compares evaporation and boiling for a particular liquid (e.g. water). Complete the table by filling in the missing words.

Evaporation	Boiling
Liquid changes to gas at temperatures .... boiling point.	Liquid changes to gas at the boiling point.
No bubbles are formed.	Boiling produces bubbles .... the liquid.
This can take place at .... temperature.	Boiling takes place at a .... temperature.
This leads to .... of temperature.	The temperature remains ....
This takes place at the .... of a liquid.	Boiling takes place throughout a liquid.

[5]

Conduction

Student's Book pages 150–153 | Syllabus learning objectives 2.3.1.1;
SUPPLEMENT 2.3.1.2–2.3.1.4

1 **a** Circle the **two** best thermal conductors from the list below.

air   copper   rubber   steel   wood   wool   [1]

b Suggest a common feature of the materials identified as the best thermal conductors.

.... [1]

c What term can you use as the opposite of good conductors? Give one example of such a material.

....

.... [2]

d Explain why it is sensible to make a cooking pot from a metal and its handle from either plastic or wood.

....

.... [2]

e In an experiment, two different test tubes are heated. Both test tubes have solid butter at the bottom. The test tube labelled A has water, and test tube B has metal pellets. The test tubes are heated from the top end as shown below.

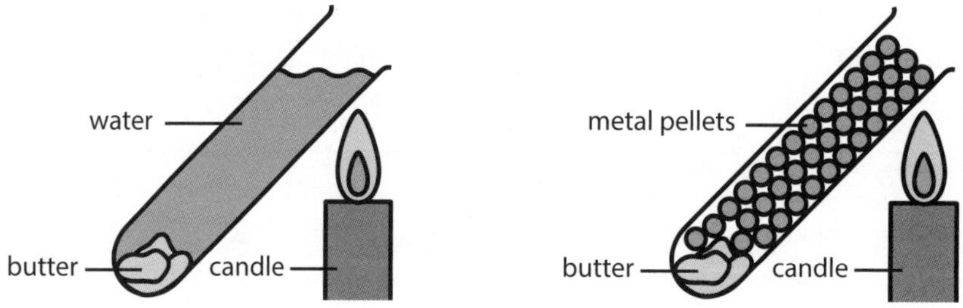

Describe in which test tube the butter would start to melt first.

....

.... [2]

2 **a** Which following term, or terms, fully explain the thermal conduction in metals? Circle your answer.

SUPPLEMENT

A lattice vibrations

B lattice vibrations, movement of free (delocalised) electrons

C lattice vibrations, movement of protons

D movement of free (delocalised) electrons [1]

b Metals are good electrical conductors and good thermal conductors. Suggest why this is.

.... [1]

c The diagram opposite shows particles within a metal. One end of the metal is hot and the other end is cold. Thermal energy is either transferred from A to B or from B to A.

Identify the direction in which thermal energy is transferred.

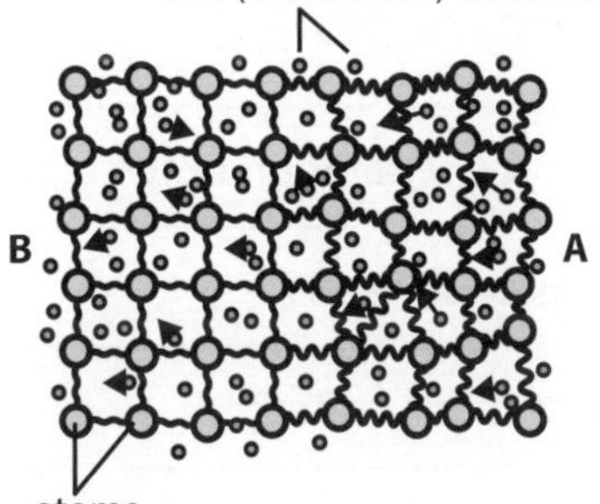

free (delocalised) electrons

atoms

.... [1]

d State why a gas such as air is a poor thermal conductor compared with a solid such as wood.

.... [1]

e State why a metal such as copper is a better thermal conductor than a solid such as wood.

.... [1]

Convection

Student's Book pages 153–154 | Syllabus learning objectives 2.3.2.1–2.3.2.2

1 Complete the sentence below.

Convection is an important method of thermal energy transfer in ....

and .... In ...., convection cannot take

place because the particles are held tightly together. [3]

2 ▸ This question is about convection in a liquid such as water.

Place a tick under the appropriate column for each quantity when water is heated in a beaker with a Bunsen burner.

What happens to ...	Increases	Decreases	Stays the same
the average separation between water molecules?			
the density of water?			
the mass of the water?			
the temperature of the water?			

[4]

3 ▸ A light piece of paper is held over a table lamp. The bulb of the lamp is very hot. Explain why the paper over the lamp will be lifted upwards.

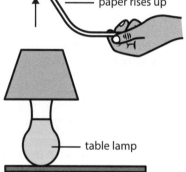

paper rises up

table lamp

....

....

....

[2]

Radiation

Student's Book pages 154–157 | Syllabus learning objectives 2.3.3.1–2.3.3.3;
`SUPPLEMENT` 2.3.3.4–2.3.3.9

1 ▸ **a** The Sun is a hot glowing ball of gas in space. Almost all of the energy arriving at the Earth's surface comes from the Sun.

What is the method of transfer of energy from the Sun to the Earth? Circle your answer.

A conduction　　**B** convection　　**C** nuclear　　**D** radiation　　[1]

b The diagram opposite shows a small camp fire.

State the methods of heat transfer to points A and B.

> **TIP**
>
> Air is a poor conductor of thermal energy.

A

B

....

.... [2]

c Thermal radiation is emitted by all objects. Circle the correct name of the waves responsible for this radiation.

     infrared   radio waves   sound   visible light   water waves   [1]

2 A student is investigating the absorption of infrared radiation by using three identical thermometers. The bulbs of the thermometers are painted in different colours – black, shiny white and grey.

All the thermometers are left in the room for some time and then hung out in bright sunshine for one hour. The temperatures from all three thermometers are recorded.

a Suggest why it was sensible to leave the thermometers in a room before taking them out into the bright sunshine.

....

.... [1]

b Explain the relative temperatures of the three thermometers.

....

....

....

....

.... [4]

3 One of the heating systems used in cold countries is a large liquid-filled metal tank. The tank has water, or oil, that is electrically heated during daytime. At night time, the tank is used to warm a room.

Explain the colour of the tank you would choose.

....

.... [2]

4 **a** A metal pen is placed under a hot table lamp. The pen starts to get warm and after some time reaches a constant temperature.

SUPPLEMENT

Explain why the temperature of the pen stays constant.

....

.... [2]

b The Earth receives infrared radiation from the Sun. The Earth also emits infrared radiation away from its surface. The graph opposite shows the variation of the temperature θ of the ground in a particular town after sunrise.

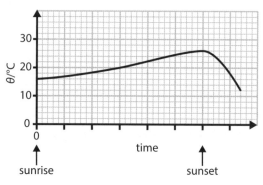

Explain why the temperature:

i rises after sunrise

....

.... [2]

ii decreases after sunset.

....

.... [2]

5 **a** The rate of emission of radiation from hot objects, similar in texture, depends on two factors. Name these two factors.

SUPPLEMENT

1 .... 2 .... [2]

b In an investigation on the emission of infrared radiation, a student is given two identical metal bottles – one is painted shiny white and the other is black.

Describe how you can demonstrate that the black bottle is a good **emitter** of infrared radiation. In your description, include:

- any additional equipment required

- the measurements you would take

- how the data collected will be used to reach a conclusion.

....

....

....

.... **[4]**

• •

Consequences of thermal energy transfer

Student's Book pages 158–161 | Syllabus learning objectives 2.3.4.1;
SUPPLEMENT 2.3.4.2

....

1 A metal cooking pan is placed over a fire. The pan contains water and some potatoes. The handle of the pan is made of metal.

a State the method by which

i thermal energy is transferred through the bottom of the pan

.... **[1]**

ii the water gets hot

.... **[1]**

    iii the potatoes get cooked.

.... [1]

b Suggest why it is not sensible to touch the end of the pan handle with bare hands while the potatoes are cooking.

....

.... [2]

2 The diagram shows a room with a heater at one end. The arrows show the direction of the movement of the air within the room when the window is closed.

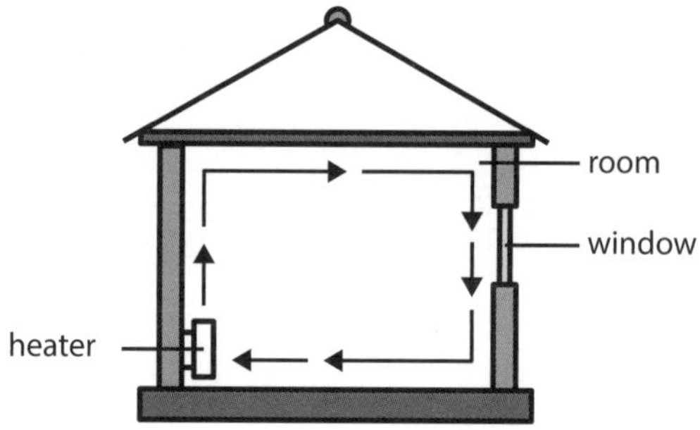

a Explain the movement of the air in the room.

....

....

....

.... [4]

b It is much colder outside the room. Suggest why it would not be sensible to open the window.

....

.... [1]

3 The purpose of a car 'radiator' is simply to remove thermal energy from the hot engine. This is done by circulating water around the engine and passing this water through the radiator. The radiator is often made of a good thermal conductor and it has 'fins' to increase the surface area which hot water passes through.

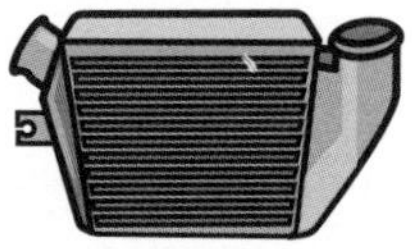

SUPPLEMENT

a Suggest a suitable thermal conductor for a car radiator.

.... [1]

b What do you think is the advantage of having fins that increase the surface area?

.... [1]

c A car radiator is at the front of a car. State one benefit of having air passing over the radiator when the car is moving.

.... [1]

4 A vacuum flask is used to keep hot liquid hot or cold liquids cold. The diagram shows the inner parts of a vacuum flask.

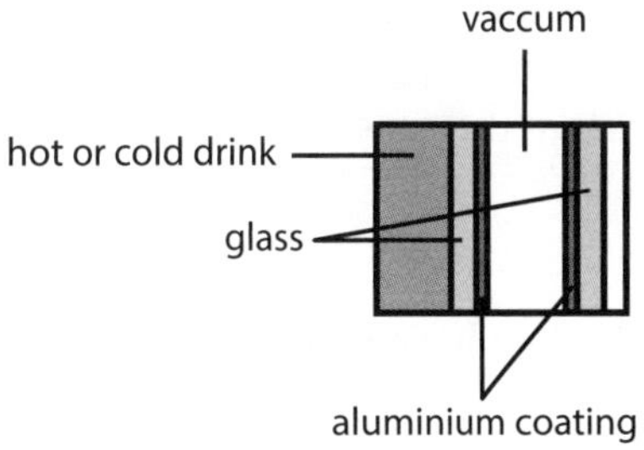

Explain how the liquid inside the flask is hot for longer because of the silver (aluminium) coating of the double glass walls and the vacuum between the glass walls.

vaccum

hot or cold drink

glass

aluminium coating

....

....

.... [3]

Waves

Student's Book pages 170–176 | Syllabus learning objectives 3.1.1–3.1.8;
SUPPLEMENT 3.1.9–3.1.10

··

1 A long spring is stretched out on level-ground and fixed at one end. The other end of the spring is repeatedly shaken at right angles to the spring.

a State the type of wave motion this will generate.

.... [1]

b State what the vibrations transfer from one end of the spring to its other end.

.... [1]

c The diagram below shows the displacement–distance graph for the wave on the spring.

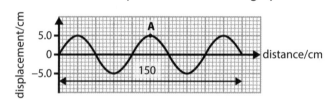

Determine the amplitude and wavelength of the wave.

TIP
The wavelength is the distance between adjacent peaks (or troughs).

amplitude = ... cm   [1]

wavelength = ... cm   [2]

d The frequency of the wave is 3.0 Hz. What does this mean in terms of the motion of point A?

.... [1]

e Describe how you can produce another type of wave motion on the stretched spring. In your description name the type of motion.

....
.... [2]

f   Circle all the waves that can be described as being transverse waves.

water waves   sound   seismic P–waves   light   seismic S–waves   [1]

2   Water waves in a ripple tank have wavelength 1.2 cm and frequency 20 Hz.

a   Calculate the speed v of the water waves.

TIP
The speed is required in cm/s, so leave the wavelength in cm.

$v =$ .... cm/s   [3]

b   The frequency of the waves is increased. Explain the effect this would have on the speed of the waves and their wavelength.

....

....

....   [3]

3   **a**   Calculate the frequency f of a wave with speed 3000 m/s and wavelength 6.0 mm.

TIP
1 mm = 0.001 m or 10^{-3} m.

$f =$ .... Hz   [3]

b   There are two types of wave motion – longitudinal waves and transverse waves. What is common for **both** of these types of waves? Circle your answer.

   A   They are vibrations in space.

   B   They transfer matter between two points.

   C   Vibrations are parallel to the direction of propagation.

   D   Vibrations are perpendicular to the direction of propagation.   [1]

4 **a** The diagram shows a ripple tank used to demonstrate the properties of water waves.

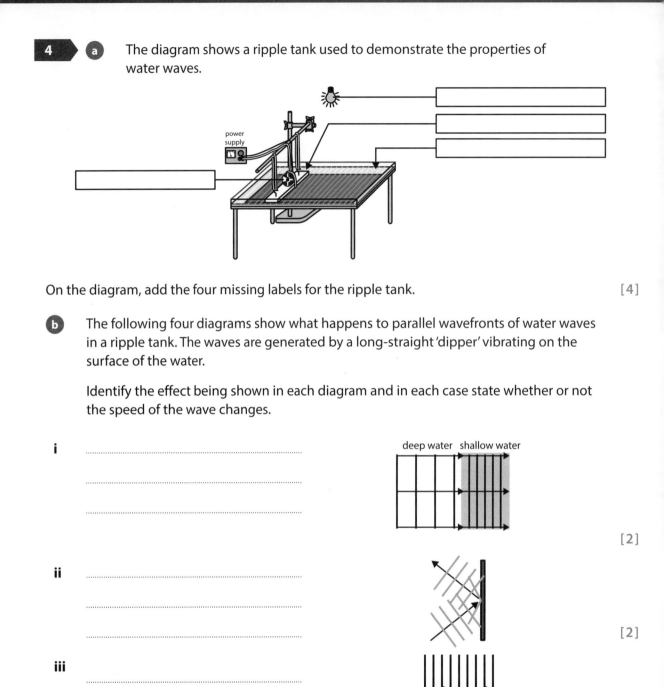

On the diagram, add the four missing labels for the ripple tank. [4]

b The following four diagrams show what happens to parallel wavefronts of water waves in a ripple tank. The waves are generated by a long-straight 'dipper' vibrating on the surface of the water.

Identify the effect being shown in each diagram and in each case state whether or not the speed of the wave changes.

i ....

....

....

[2]

ii ....

....

....

[2]

iii ....

....

....

[2]

iv ....

....

....

[2]

5

UPPLEMENT

For questions **4(b)(iii)** and **4(b)(iv)**, describe how you could increase the effects shown in the ripple tank.

....

....

[2]

• •

Reflection of light

Student's Book pages 180–183 | Syllabus learning objectives 3.2.1.1–3.2.1.3;
SUPPLEMENT 3.2.1.4

....

1 The diagram opposite shows a ray of light from a laser that is incident at a plane mirror.

Complete the diagram by:

• drawing a normal

• drawing the reflected ray

• marking the angle of incidence i and the angle of reflection r.

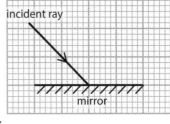

[3]

2 A person is looking at their reflected image in a plane mirror.

The list on the following page shows some statements that may be correct about the characteristics of the image.

Tick ✓ the ones that are correct in this situation.

Possible characteristics of the image	Tick here if correct
The image is larger than the object.	
The image is same distance behind the mirror as the object is in front.	
The image is same size as the object.	
The image is laterally inverted (left appears as right).	
The image is on the surface of the mirror.	
The image is real.	
The image is virtual.	

[4]

3

SUPPLEMENT

An incomplete ray diagram is shown for locating the image of an object formed in a plane mirror.

a Complete the ray diagram. On the diagram indicate:

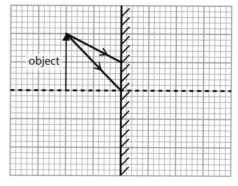

- the location of the image

- the height of the image

- where you would place your eye to see the image.

[4]

TIP
You can determine the top of the image by extrapolating the two reflected rays.

b The object has height 1.0 cm and is placed 2.0 cm in front of the mirror.

i What is the separation between the image and the object? Explain your answer.

....

.... [2]

ii State the height of the image.

height of image =... cm [1]

Refraction of light

Student's Book pages 183–184 | Syllabus learning objectives 3.2.2.1–3.2.2.3

1 The diagram below shows a ray of light from a laser that is incident at the surface of a rectangular glass block. The ray emerging from the block is also shown.

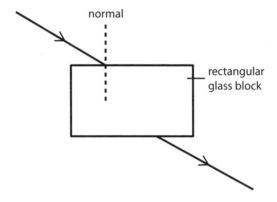

The diagram is drawn to scale.

a Draw the refracted ray through the glass block. [1]

b Use the diagram to measure the angle of incidence i and the angle of refraction r using a protractor.

$i =$ .... ° $r =$ .... ° [2]

c State why refraction occurs as light travels from air into glass.

.... [1]

2 A ray of light enters different-shaped glass blocks. In each case, complete the path of the light through the glass block.

a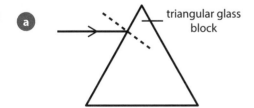

b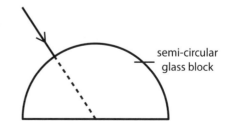

[4]

3 A person is looking at the bottom of a swimming pool and notices that the pool looks much shallower than its actual depth. This is an illusion because of the refraction of light at the water–air boundary.

The diagram below shows the path of just one ray of light from the bottom of the pool.

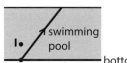

bottom of the pool

The position of the image of the bottom of the pool is marked with the letter I.

a Complete the diagram to show the ray entering the eye. [1]

b From the way the light is refracted at the water–air boundary, state the relative speed of light in water and in air.

.... [1]

● ●

Refractive index and critical angle

Student's Book pages pages 185–190 | Syllabus learning objectives 3.2.2.4–3.2.2.5;
SUPPLEMENT 3.2.2.6–3.2.2.9

....

1 **a** A ray of light in water travelling towards the water–air boundary is shown opposite.

Complete the diagram to show the critical angle c for water. Include any necessary labels.

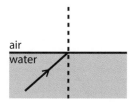

[3]

b State what happens to a ray of light when the angle of incidence is:

i less than c

.... [1]

ii greater than c.

.... [1]

c What is the name given to the phenomenon mentioned in **(b)(ii)**? Circle your answer.

A total internal diffraction   **C** total internal reflection

B total internal energy   **D** total internal refraction [1]

2 The critical angle for glass is 42°.

a The diagram opposite shows the path of a ray of light for a particular triangular glass block. Explain the path of the ray of light in the glass block.

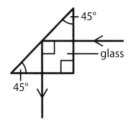

....

.... [2]

b The diagram below shows two glass prisms used in a pair of binoculars. Complete the path of the light ray shown.

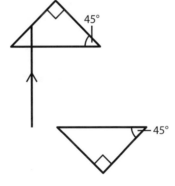

[2]

3 The table below shows the refractive index of some transparent materials.

Material	Diamond	Glass	Ice	Quartz	Water
Refractive index	2.42	1.52	1.31	1.54	1.33

a The speed of light in a vacuum is c. The speed of light in a transparent material is v. Write an equation for the refractive index n of the material.

[1]

b Without any calculation, explain for which material shown in the table that the speed of light in the material is the slowest.

....

.... [2]

c Calculate the speed v of light in ice.

$v =$... m/s [3]

4 A thin beam of light from a ray box passes through a transparent material. The angle of incidence i and the angle of refraction r are recorded for a range of i values.

SUPPLEMENT

a Explain why a graph of i against r will not be a straight-line through the origin.

....

.... [2]

b For $i = 60.0°$, the value of $r = 34.2°$.

Calculate the refractive index n to two decimal places and identify the material from the table given in question **1**.

$n =$... [3]

5 **a** The refractive index of vegetable oil is 1.47. Calculate the critical angle c for this oil.

SUPPLEMENT

$c =$...° [3]

b Optical fibres are used in telecommunications and are replacing copper wires. Explain how an optical fibre works. You may support your answer with a suitable diagram.

....

....

.... [3]

Lenses and dispersion

Student's Book pages 191–196 | Syllabus learning objectives 3.2.3.1–3.2.3.5;
SUPPLEMENT 3.2.3.6–3.2.3.8 ; 3.2.4.1–3.2.4.2; SUPPLEMENT 3.2.4.3

⋯⋯⋯⋯⋯⋯⋯⋯⋯⋯⋯⋯⋯⋯⋯⋯⋯⋯⋯⋯⋯⋯

1 ▸ Complete the three definitions below.

a The principal axis of a lens is a line of symmetry passing through the

.... of the lens. [1]

b The principal focus (focal point) of a converging lens is a ....

at which rays of light .... to the principal axis converge to after

passing through the lens. [2]

c A parallel beam of light incident at a diverging lens emerges as a

.... beam after passing through the lens. This ....

beam appears to come from the principal focus of the lens. [1]

2 ▸ **a** The diagram opposite shows two rays of light
passing through a thin converging lens.

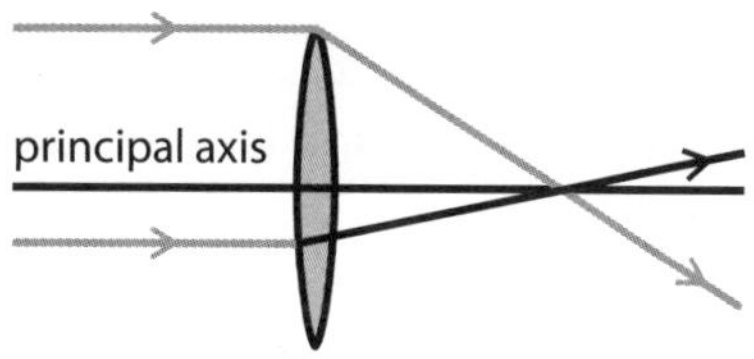

On the diagram show the principal focus (focal
point) with a letter F and indicate the focal length f
of the lens.

[2]

b The Sun is a very distant object. Almost parallel rays of light from the Sun arrive at
the Earth.

You are given a piece of white card and a converging lens of unknown focal length f.

Describe how you could use the white card on a sunny day to determine f.

....

....

.... [3]

3 A converging lens is used to form a sharp image of a light bulb (**object**) on a screen. In the diagram below, the object is shown by an upright arrow and labelled O. The principal focus on either side of the lens is marked by the letter F.

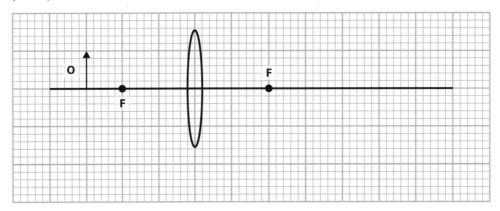

a Draw two rays of light from the top of the object that pass through the converging lens. [2]

b Draw the position of the image. [1]

c Circle the words below that correctly describe the characteristics of the image formed on the screen.

diminished   inverted   magnified (enlarged)

real   virtual   upright   [3]

4 A large converging lens is being used as a magnifying glass for reading small text in a book.

SUPPLEMENT

In the diagram below, the object is shown by an upright arrow and the principal focus on either side of the lens is marked by the letter F.

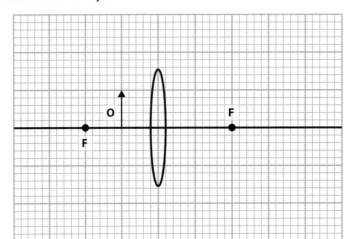

TIP

The image can only be seen if the eye looks through the lens.

a Use the diagram to draw a ray diagram for locating the image. [3]

b Describe the characteristics of the image.

....

.... [2]

5 A diverging lens is used to form an image of an object. The image is always virtual.

What is another characteristic of the image? Circle your answer.

A The image can be either diminished or magnified.

B The image is always diminished.

C The image is always inverted.

diverging lens

D The image is always magnified. [1]

6 Explain in terms of seeing distant and close objects what is meant by short-sightedness
SUPPLEMENT and long-sightedness. For each condition, describe how it can be corrected by placing
a single lens in front of the eye.

....

....

....

....

.... [5]

7 **a** Describe how you can demonstrate the dispersion of white light in the laboratory.

....

.... [2]

b State how the wavelength of yellow light compares with the wavelength of red light.

.... [1]

c List blue, red and green colours of light in order of increasing frequency.

.... [1]

d The dispersion of white light produces seven coloured lights. List the colours of the
light in the order of increasing wavelength.

.... [1]

(e) What is monochromatic light? Circle your answer.

A Light of a single frequency.

B Light of the same amplitude,

C Light that changes direction.

D Light with the same speed. [1]

Electromagnetic waves

Student's Book pages 201–207 | Syllabus learning objectives 3.3.1–3.3.4;
SUPPLEMENT 3.3.6

1 This question is about the main regions of the electromagnetic spectrum.

(a) A student has listed below the main regions of the electromagnetic spectrum in order of **increasing** frequency.

radio waves; microwaves; infrared; ultraviolet; visible light; X-rays; gamma rays

Two main regions in the list are not in the correct sequence. What is the error, and suggest how this error can be resolved?

....

.... [2]

(b) State which main region of electromagnetic waves has the shortest wavelength.

.... [1]

(c) List all the main regions of electromagnetic waves that have a wavelength longer than that of infrared waves.

.... [1]

(d) List all the main regions of electromagnetic waves that have a frequency greater than that of visible light.

.... [1]

2 The electromagnetic radiation emitted by a distant exploded star is being observed from the Earth. The star has been known to emit all types of electromagnetic radiation.

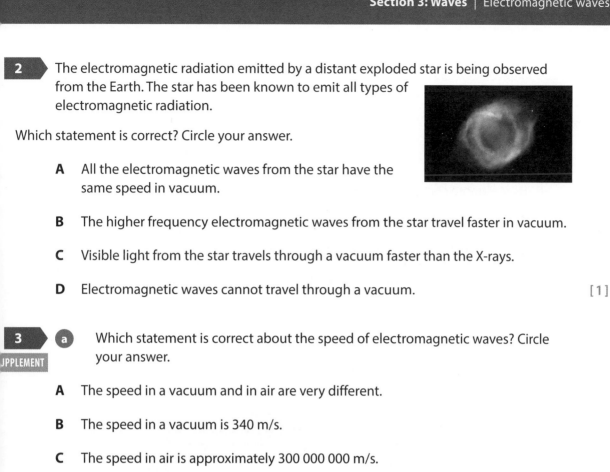

Which statement is correct? Circle your answer.

A   All the electromagnetic waves from the star have the same speed in vacuum.

B   The higher frequency electromagnetic waves from the star travel faster in vacuum.

C   Visible light from the star travels through a vacuum faster than the X-rays.

D   Electromagnetic waves cannot travel through a vacuum.   [1]

3 **a** Which statement is correct about the speed of electromagnetic waves? Circle your answer.

SUPPLEMENT

A   The speed in a vacuum and in air are very different.

B   The speed in a vacuum is 340 m/s.

C   The speed in air is approximately 300 000 000 m/s.

D   The speed depends on its wavelength.   [1]

b Calculate the distance travelled by radio waves in 1 minute.

> **TIP**
>
> Radio waves are electromagnetic waves.

distance = ... m   [3]

c The circumference of the Earth is about 40 000 km.

Calculate the time it would take for light to travel this distance.

time = ... s   [3]

4 Electromagnetic waves have many uses.

Each row in the table below shows some of the uses for a particular type of electromagnetic wave.

A	Astronomy and radio frequency identification (RFID).
B	Remote controllers for digital devices and thermal imaging.
C	Detecting fake bank notes and sterilising water.
D	Medical scanning and security scanners.
E	Sterilising food and detecting cancer.
F	Satellite television and mobile phones (cell phones).
G	Photography and illumination.

In the table below, identify the correct row for each type of electromagnetic wave. One has already been done for you.

Electromagnetic wave	The correct row for uses
Radio waves	
Microwaves	
Infrared	
Visible light	
Ultraviolet	
X-rays	
Gamma rays	E

[6]

5 In each case below, identify the type electromagnetic radiation that may have caused the harmful effect in patients being treated at a hospital after excessive exposure to a particular type of radiation.

a External burns to the hand. .... [1]

b Internal scarring of the hand caused by internal heating. .... [1]

c Mutation of cells in the lung. .... [1]

d Skin cancer on the arm. .... [1]

Communicating with electromagnetic waves

Student's Book pages 207–209 | Syllabus learning objectives 3.3.5;
SUPPLEMENT 3.3.7–3.3.10

1 Artificial satellites are used for phone communication. The diagram opposite shows satellites in two different types of orbits – low Earth orbit and high-altitude geostationary orbit.

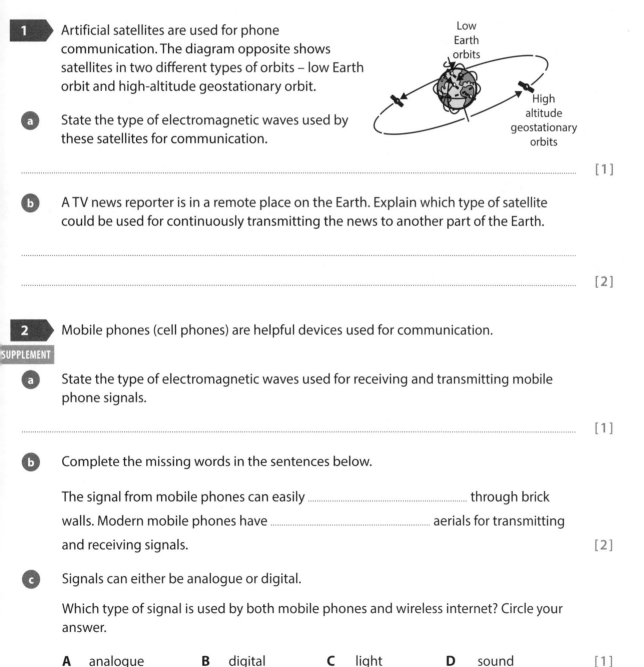

Low Earth orbits

High altitude geostationary orbits

a State the type of electromagnetic waves used by these satellites for communication.

.... [1]

b A TV news reporter is in a remote place on the Earth. Explain which type of satellite could be used for continuously transmitting the news to another part of the Earth.

....

.... [2]

2 Mobile phones (cell phones) are helpful devices used for communication.

SUPPLEMENT

a State the type of electromagnetic waves used for receiving and transmitting mobile phone signals.

.... [1]

b Complete the missing words in the sentences below.

The signal from mobile phones can easily .... through brick

walls. Modern mobile phones have .... aerials for transmitting

and receiving signals. [2]

c Signals can either be analogue or digital.

Which type of signal is used by both mobile phones and wireless internet? Circle your answer.

A analogue   **B** digital   **C** light   **D** sound   [1]

3 **a** Here are some statements about Bluetooth technology. Place a tick ✓ in the last column if the statement is correct for Bluetooth.

SUPPLEMENT

Statement	Place a tick ✓ here if correct ...
Bluetooth can exchange information between digital devices.	
Bluetooth is short-range.	
Bluetooth signals cannot pass through brick walls.	
Bluetooth uses analogue signals.	
Bluetooth uses microwaves or low-energy radio waves.	
Bluetooth uses optical fibres.	

[6]

b State one example of Bluetooth technology that may be used by a mobile phone (cell phone).

.... [1]

4 **a** Describe what is meant by a digital signal. Draw a diagram to illustrate your answer.

SUPPLEMENT

.... [2]

b A few decades ago, digital devices such as computers and mobile phones (cell phones) were large and bulky. Nowadays, the opposite is true.

State at least two other advantages of the digital devices named above.

....

.... [2]

Sound and ultrasound

Student's Book pages 213–220 | Syllabus learning objectives 3.4.1–3.4.9;
SUPPLEMENT 3.4.10–3.4.12

....

1 ▶ Describe a simple method of creating a sound that can be heard.

In your answer, describe the nature of sound waves and a typical value for the frequency of the emitted sound.

....

....

.... [3]

2 ▶

a Explain why sound created on a distant planet cannot be heard on the Earth, no matter how sensitive our detecting devices are.

....

.... [2]

b A person at a distance of 200 m creates a loud sound by banging together two blocks of wood. The speed of sound in air is 340 m/s. The student wishes to directly measure the time it would take for sound to travel 200 m using a stopwatch.

   i Calculate the time it would take sound to travel this distance.

   time = ... s [1]

   ii Suggest why it would not be sensible to measure the time taken for sound to travel 200 m with a stopwatch.

.... [1]

3

SUPPLEMENT

A scientist is investigating the speed of sound in air and in seawater. A fixed distance of 1.0 km is used. The scientist records the time *t* taken for the sound waves to travel this distance.

The experiment is repeated four times for both air and seawater. The table below shows the data collected.

t/ s for air	3.00	2.95	3.08	2.90	
t/ s for seawater	0.67	0.72	0.66	0.70	

a Determine the average times for air and seawater. Write the values, to two decimal places, in the last column. [2]

b Use the information above to deduce whether the speed of sound is greater in air or in seawater.

....

.... [2]

c Sound travelling through air, and in seawater, produces compression and rarefaction regions. Explain what is meant by compressions and rarefactions.

....

.... [2]

4 A loudspeaker is placed next to a wall. There is another wall opposite at a distance of 6.0 m. The loudspeaker creates a single loud bleep. The sound waves are reflected at the walls.

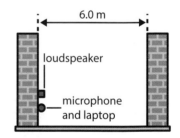

A microphone is placed next to the loudspeaker. A laptop connected to the microphone shows the following pattern for the sound detected.

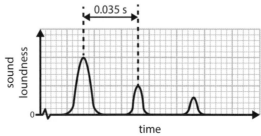

a What is another term for the reflection of sound?

.... [1]

b Explain why several 'peaks' are detected by the microphone.

....

.... [2]

c The time between the adjacent peaks is 0.035 s.

i Explain why the distance travelled by the sound is 12 m in this time.

.... [1]

ii Calculate the speed of sound.

> **TIP**
>
> Use the information provided in (c)(i) to calculate the speed.

speed =.. m/s [2]

d State how you could make the initial bleep from the loudspeaker:

i louder

.... [1]

ii have a higher pitch.

.... [1]

5 Ultrasound is used in medical imaging of the body.

a State a typical frequency for ultrasound in kHz. .... [1]

SUPPLEMENT **b** A patient is having an ultrasound scan of the eye to determine the length L of their eyeball.

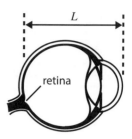

The time taken for the ultrasound to travel from the front of the eye to the retina and back again to the front of the eye is 3.2×10^{-5} s. The speed of ultrasound in the eye is 1500 m/s.

Calculate the length L of the patient's eyeball.

$L =$.. m   [4]

Magnetism

Student's Book pages 228-234 | Syllabus learning objectives 4.1.1–4.1.9;
SUPPLEMENT 4.1.10–4.1.11

1 This question is about bar magnets.

a Complete the sentences below.

A permanent bar magnet has two magnetic poles, a .... pole

and a .... pole. The space around the bar magnet is

surrounded by a .... field. Another magnet placed in this field will

experience a ....

b A bar magnet is fixed at the bottom of a vertical plastic tube. Another bar magnet M is
held at the upper end of the tube as shown in the diagram.

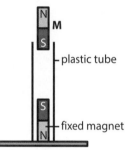

TIP

The magnets will either repel or attract
depending on the polarities of the facing poles.

i Explain what happens to the bar magnet M when it is dropped into the tube and it
gets closer to the bottom of the tube.

....

.... [2]

ii Explain what would happen to the magnet M if it was dropped with its opposite
pole facing the bottom of the tube.

....

.... [2]

c A sample of soft-iron can be made into a temporary magnet by placing it in an external magnetic field. This process is known as *induced magnetism*. The two diagrams below show the same soft-iron sample placed close to the south-seeking (S) pole of the permanent magnet **(i)**, and then close to the north-seeking (N) pole of the permanent magnet **(ii)**.

soft-iron   soft-iron

N   S   N   S

(i)   **(ii)**

Complete both diagrams by marking the induced poles of the soft-iron sample.   [2]

d A student correctly draws a single magnetic field line for a bar magnet; this is shown in the diagram below. The direction of the magnetic field was determined using a magnetic compass.

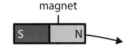

magnet

S   N

i Complete the magnetic field pattern for the bar magnet. You must sketch this pattern using at least four more magnetic field lines.   [2]

ii Identify the north-seeking (N) pole and the south-seeking (S) pole of the bar magnet on the diagram.   [1]

iii Describe how you can directly show the magnetic field pattern around this bar magnet.

....

....   [2]

2 **a** **i** In the list below, there are two magnetic materials, the remaining four are non-magnetic materials. Circle the four non-magnetic materials.

aluminium   copper   iron   plastic   steel   wood   [1]

ii State the major difference between magnetic materials and non-magnetic materials.

....

.... [1]

b A temporary magnet can be made from a magnetic material such as soft-iron. State a magnetic material that can be used to make a permanent magnet.

.... [1]

3 An electromagnet can be made by inserting a soft-iron rod into an insulated copper coil and connecting the coil to a power supply.

a Describe how an electromagnet differs from a permanent magnet.

....

.... [2]

b In a car scrapyard, heavy cars are lifted using a large electromagnet connected to a crane. Suggest two advantages of using an electromagnet in a car scrapyard.

....

.... [2]

4 **a** Two magnets will either attract or repel each other. Which statement best describes the reason why two magnets will exert a force on each other? Circle your answer.

SUPPLEMENT

A The magnetic fields of the magnets interact.

B The magnets are affected by gravitational field of the Earth.

C The magnets are electrically charged.

D The magnets are made from steel. [1]

b   The diagram opposite shows the magnetic field pattern for a horseshoe magnet.

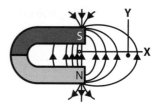

Describe how the relative strength of the magnetic field at X compares with that at Y. Explain your answer.

....

.... [2]

Electric charge

Student's Book pages 237–245 | Syllabus learning objectives 4.2.1.1–4.2.1.6;
SUPPLEMENT 4.2.1.7–4.2.1.10

1   Electric charge can either be positive (+) or negative (−). The forces between charged objects can either be attractive or repulsive.

a   In the diagram below, state whether there is an attractive force, or a repulsive force, between the charged objects.

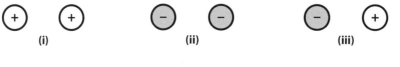

(i) ....   (ii) ....   (iii) ....

[3]

b   Formulate a rule for the type of force using the terms 'like charges' and 'unlike charges'.

.... [1]

2   A piece of cloth is used to polish a plastic table. Initially, the cloth and the plastic table are both electrically neutral.

a   State the relationship between the amount of negative charge and the amount of positive charge on any insulator that is electrically neutral.

.... [1]

b After polishing the table, the cloth acquires a positive charge.

> **TIP**
>
> The friction between two insulators helps to transfer electrons between the insulators.

i Explain, in terms of electrons, how the cloth becomes positively charged.

....

.... [2]

ii State the type of charge on the polished table.

.... [1]

3 The simple circuit opposite is used by a student to identify whether a material is an electrical conductor, or an electrical insulator. The 'test' material is placed between the contacts P and N.

a Explain the state of the lamp:

i when an insulator is placed between the contacts

....

.... [2]

ii when a conductor is placed between the contacts.

....

.... [2]

b In the list below, circle the three best electrical conductors.

aluminium   copper   gold   oil   plastic   silk   wood   [1]

4 **a** What is the unit for electric charge? Circle your answer.

SUPPLEMENT

A ampere   **B** coulomb   **C** hooke   **D** newton   [1]

b A large vertical metal plate is electrically charged. It is not known if the plate has a negative, or a positive charge. The space around the metal plate is occupied by an *electric field*.

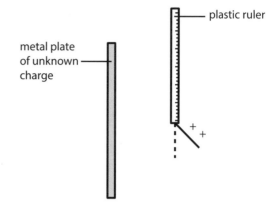

A tiny **positively** charged gold foil, at the end of a vertical plastic ruler, is brought close to the metal plate. The metal foil deflects away from the metal plate as shown in the diagram.

i Explain what is meant by an electric field.

.... [1]

ii What is the direction of the electric field and the charge on the metal plate? Give a reason for your answer.

....

....

.... [3]

c Some incomplete electric field patterns are shown below.

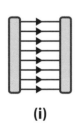
(i)

(ii)

(iii)

> **TIP**
>
> The direction of an electric field at a point is the direction in which a free positive charge would move at that point.

Identify the electric field pattern for:

- a negative point charge .... [1]

- a positive point charge .... [1]

- two oppositely charged parallel plates. .... [1]

Electric current

Student's Book pages 245–248 | Syllabus learning objectives 4.2.2.1–4.2.2.4;
SUPPLEMENT 4.2.2.5–4.2.2.6

1 **a** Some students confuse electric charge and electric current. These quantities are related to each other, but they are not the same.

Electric current is related to the flow of which quantity? Circle your answer.

A charge   **B** energy   **C** force   **D** time   [1]

b Which particles move in the copper wire of an electric circuit when there is conduction (or a current)? Circle your answer.

A atoms   **B** electrons   **C** ions   **D** protons   [1]

c State one instance in which a digital ammeter would be preferable to an analogue ammeter.

.... [1]

2 The three graphs below show the variation of electric current with time.

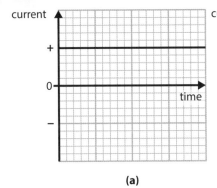
(a)

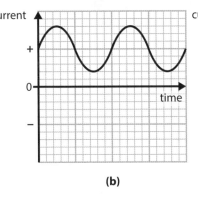
(b)

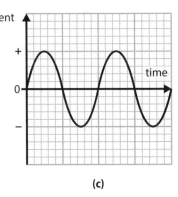
(c)

In each case, state whether the current is direct or alternating. Give a reason for each answer.

(a) ....

....

(b) ....

....

(c) ....

.... [6]

3

a Complete the definition for electric current below.

SUPPLEMENT

Electric current is defined as the .... that passes a point in a

circuit .... unit time. [1]

b In the circuit opposite, the ammeter shows a constant reading of 0.50 A.

i State the **relationship** between the charge Q and the time t taken for this charge to flow past a point in a circuit.

....

.... [2]

ii Calculate the charge Q moving past any point in the circuit in a time of 20 s.

$Q =$ .... C [3]

iii Using either the term 'clockwise' and/or the term 'anticlockwise', state the direction of:

• the electron flow in the circuit

.... [1]

• the conventional current.

.... [1]

c Calculate the current I in milliamperes (mA) in a battery charger when the charge flow in a time of 60 s is 15 C.

TIP
The prefix milli means 1000 times smaller. So, 1 A = 1000 mA.

$I =$ .... A [3]

Electromotive force and potential difference

Student's Book pages 248–250 | Syllabus learning objectives 4.2.3.1–4.2.3.5;
SUPPLEMENT 4.2.3.6–4.2.3.7

....

1 **a** Which statement is correct about electromotive force (e.m.f.)? Circle your answer.

A It is related to the force experienced by charges in a complete circuit.

B It is the electrical work done in moving a unit charge in a complete circuit.

C It is the total current in a complete circuit.

D It is the work done by the complete circuit. [1]

b Circle all the items in the list below that are commonly used to define **both** electromotive force (e.m.f.) and potential difference (p.d.).

current   force   unit charge   unit mass   unit volume   work done

[2]

c Name two types of meters that can be used to measure the potential difference across a component in an electrical circuit.

.... [2]

d A student is measuring the potential difference across a length of wire. The circuit diagram drawn by the student is shown opposite.

What is the mistake made by the student? Suggest how you can correct this mistake.

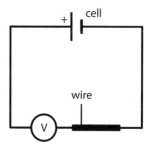

....

.... [2]

2 The e.m.f. E of a cell can be calculated using the equation: $E = \dfrac{W}{Q}$.

SUPPLEMENT

a Identify the quantities represented by the letters W and E.

W: .... Q: .... [2]

b The e.m.f. of a cell is 1.4 V.
Complete the table below.

$Q/$ C	1.0	2.0	10	100
$W/$ J				

[4]

3 A small heater consists of a coiled copper wire. This heater and a lamp are connected in series to a power supply. The electromotive force (e.m.f.) of the power supply is 12 V. The current in the heater is 2.0 A.

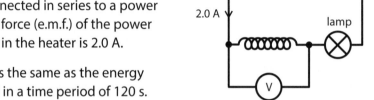

The electrical work done, which is the same as the energy transferred by the heater, is 960 J in a time period of 120 s.

a Show that the charge flow in the heater in 120 s is 240 C.

TIP
You must clearly show all the steps of the calculations because the answer is given.

[2]

b Calculate the potential difference (p.d.) V across the heater.

$V =$ .... V [3]

c Explain why your value for V is not the same as the e.m.f of the power supply.

....

.... [2]

Resistance

Student's Book pages 250–257 | Syllabus learning objectives 4.2.4.1–4.2.4.3;
SUPPLEMENT 4.2.4.4–4.2.4.5

···

1 A student is given the task of determining the resistance of a pencil lead. The ends of the pencil are exposed as shown.

Describe an experiment for this task. In your description, include:

• the equipment you would use

• the measurements you need to take

• how the data collected will be used.

....

....

....

....

.... [4]

2 The table opposite. shows some data collected by a student investigating the resistance of an electrical component.

V/V	2.0	4.0	6.0
I/ A	1.8	2.5	3.2
R/Ω			

a Complete the table by determining the resistance of the component. Write each calculated value to two significant figures. [3]

b Use the completed table to suggest the variation of R with V.

.... [1]

3 **a** The circuit shown opposite is used by a teacher to demonstrate how the resistance of a wire of a given material depends on its length.

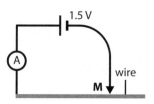

As the movable contact M is moved to the right, the current in the circuit slowly decreases.

Explain how the resistance of the wire depends on its length.

....

....   [2]

b The table below has some statements about a wire made from nickel.

Insert a tick ✓ in the last column if the statement is correct.   [4]

Statement	Place your tick ✓ here if correct …
A thicker wire has less resistance.	
Shorter length of wire has less resistance.	
The resistance of wire decreases as the current in it is increased.	
The resistance of wire increases as the potential difference is decreased.	

4 A current–voltage (*I–V*) graph is useful in identifying an electrical component.

SUPPLEMENT A resistor, at room temperature, is connected in series with an ammeter and it also has a voltmeter connected across it.

a Describe how you can change the potential difference (voltage) across the resistor in order to get data for an *I-V* graph.

....   [1]

b The *I–V* graph for the resistor is shown.

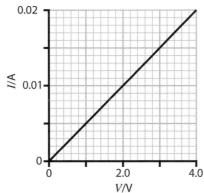

i State the relationship between *I* and *V*.

.... [1]

ii Show that the resistance of the resistor is constant by determining the resistance at 2.0 V and 4.0 V.

[4]

5 The *I–V* graph for a filament lamp is shown opposite.

SUPPLEMENT

Describe how the resistance of the filament lamp depends on the potential difference *V* across it. You are not expected to do any calculations.

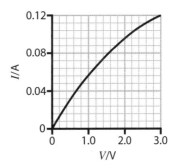

....

....

[2]

6 A student has the following short statements about a particular diode.

SUPPLEMENT

- It only conducts in one direction.

- It starts to conduct around 0.6 V.

- Beyond 0.6 V, the current increases rapidly – its resistance decreases as the p.d. increases.

Use the statements above to sketch the I–V graph for this diode.

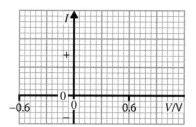

[3]

7 **a** The resistance of 0.90 m long nichrome-wire of a given cross-sectional area has
SUPPLEMENT resistance of 18 Ω.

Calculate the resistance R of a 0.60 m length of this wire.

$R =$ .... Ω [3]

b Calculate the resistance R of 0.90 m long nichrome-wire that has half the cross-sectional area of the wire in **(a)**.

$R =$ .... Ω [3]

Energy and power

Student's Book pages 257–260 | Syllabus learning objectives 4.2.5.1–4.2.5.4

....

1 A simple circuit consists of a cell that is connected in series with a resistor and a filament lamp.

a State the source of the electrical energy.

.... [1]

b Name one component that energy is transferred to by the circuit.

.... [1]

c The components connected to the cell may become warm. In such situations, where is the internal (**thermal**) energy of the components transferred to? Circle your answer.

A   the cell   **C**   the meters

B   the connecting wires   **D**   the surroundings   [1]

2 An LED-lamp is rated as 2.3 W.

TIP
Remember 1 W = 1 J per second

a State the energy transferred by the lamp in a time of 1.0 s.

.... [1]

b Calculate the energy transferred by the lamp when it is operated for 1.0 hour.

TIP
There are 60 minutes in 1 hour and 60 seconds in 1 minute.

energy transferred = ... J   [2]

c The lamp is connected to a 230 V supply. Calculate the current in the lamp.

current = ... A   [3]

3 An appliance of resistance $4.0\,\Omega$ is connected to a 12 V supply.

a Calculate the current I in the appliance.

$I =$... A   [3]

b Calculate the power P transferred by the appliance.

$P =$ .... W   [3]

c The kilowatt-hour (kW h) is an alternative unit for energy.

i Define the kW h.

....

....   [1]

ii The cost of each kW h is 18 cents. Calculate the cost of operating the appliance for 12 hours.

cost =... cents   [3]

d Explain whether a 60 W device operated for the same period as the appliance, with the same supply, would be more costly, the same cost, or less costly.

....

....   [2]

Circuit diagrams and components

Student's Book pages 265–267 | Syllabus learning objectives 4.3.1.1;
SUPPLEMENT 4.3.1.2

 a A simple light meter can be made by connecting a cell, an ammeter and a light-dependent resistor (**LDR**) in series.

i Using the correct symbols for the components, draw a circuit diagram of this light meter.

[4]

ii The resistance of the LDR decreases as the brightness of the light incident on it **increases**. On the ammeter drawing opposite, mark the positions of the ammeter pointer for 'bright' and 'dark'.

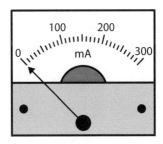

[1]

b The circuit in (**a**) can be made into a temperature-sensing circuit by swapping the LDR with a thermistor. The 'sensitivity' of the circuit can be controlled by placing a variable resistor in the circuit.

Draw the circuit symbols for a variable resistor and a thermistor.

Circuit symbol for a variable resistor	
Circuit symbol for a thermistor	

[2]

2 A potential divider circuit has two or more components in series connected to a power supply.

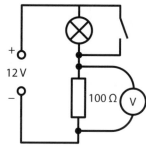

The potential divider circuit has a filament lamp and a fixed 100 Ω resistor. A switch is connected across the lamp and a voltmeter across the resistor. The e.m.f. of the power supply is 12 V.

The switch is closed.

> **TIP**
>
> With the switch closed, the lamp is 'shorted out' and the total resistance of the circuit is just 100 ohms.

a State the reading on the voltmeter.

voltmeter reading = ... V [1]

b Calculate the current in the resistor.

current = ... A [3]

c The switch is now opened.

The lamp is lit and the voltmeter reading decreases. State whether the resistance of the circuit has increased, stayed the same, or decreased.

.... [1]

3 **a** This question is about identifying electrical components in a circuit. You are not expected to have knowledge of this circuit.

Identify the components A, B, C and D.

A: ....

B: ....

C: ....

D: ....

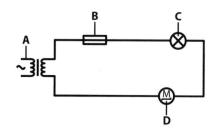

[4]

b   Complete the table below by either naming the circuit component or drawing the correct circuit symbol for the component.

Component	Circuit symbol
	—|¦----|¦—
	—[G]—
Heater	
Magnetising coil	
	⊥▭⊤

[5]

4   A diode is a component that conducts in one direction only. A light emitting diode (LED) is a special diode that emits light of a particular colour when it is conducting.

conducts this way
→

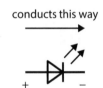

The circuit below is designed by a student as a simple polarity-checker for cells, batteries and power supplies.

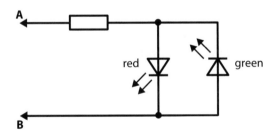

a   State which LED is lit when A is positive and B is negative.

.... [1]

b   State which LED is lit when A is negative and B is positive.

.... [1]

Series and parallel circuits

Student's Book pages 267–273 | Syllabus learning objectives 4.3.2.1–4.3.2.7;
SUPPLEMENT 4.3.2.8–4.3.2.10

1 A row of lamps, used to illuminate a courtyard, are connected in parallel rather than in series.

Which statement is correct about the lamps connected in parallel? Circle your answer.

    A Lamps connected in parallel last longer.

    B Lamps give out less light when connected in parallel.

    C Parallel circuits are easier to connect.

    D When one lamp stops working the remaining lamps are unaffected. [1]

2 The circuit opposite has three identical filament lamps connected in series.

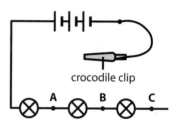

One end of the connecting wires has a crocodile clip. This clip can be connected to any of the points A, B or C.

Each cell has an electromotive force (e.m.f.) of 1.5 V.

a State the total e.m.f. of the battery of three cells.

e.m.f. =... V [1]

b The crocodile clip is connected to point C. Explain why all the lamps have the same brightness.

....

.... [2]

c The crocodile clip is now moved to point B.

The current in the circuit is 0.030 A. The brightness of the two lamps is **brighter** than the lamps in **(b)**.

    i State whether the current in the circuit is more than, the same as, or less than the current in the circuit in **(b)**.

.... [1]

ii Explain whether circuit in **(b)** or circuit in **(c)** has greater resistance.

....

.... [2]

iii Calculate the total resistance of the two lamps.

total resistance =.. Ω [3]

iv Calculate the resistance of each lamp. Show all the steps in your calculation or reasoning.

resistance of each lamp =.. Ω [3]

3 This question is about the circuit opposite. The resistors have different resistance values. One of resistors has resistance R. The electromotive force (e.m.f.) of the power supply is 9.0 V.

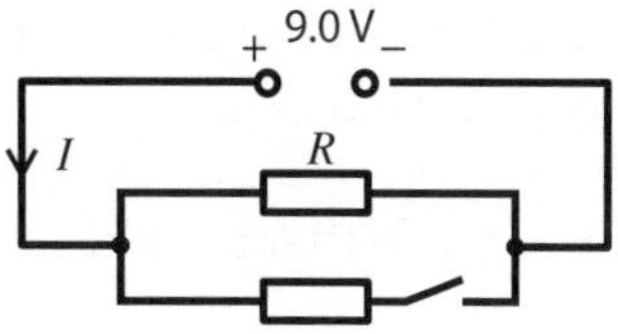

a The switch is open. The current in the circuit I is 0.15 A. Calculate the resistance R.

$R =$ .... Ω [3]

b The switch is closed, with the resistors now connected in parallel.

Without doing any calculations, state:

i how the total resistance of the circuit compares with your answer in **(a)**

.... [1]

ii how the circuit current compares with 0.15 A.

.... [1]

4 **a** For each circuit, calculate the total resistance R_C of the circuit.

i

120 Ω

120 Ω

ii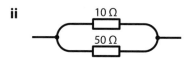

10 Ω

50 Ω

R_C for **(i)** = ... Ω R_C for **(ii)** = ... Ω   [5]

b Complete the following sentence that is applicable to both circuits in **(a)**.

The total resistance is always .... than the smaller resistance of the two resistors.   [1]

5 **a** This question is about the circuit shown opposite.

The e.m.f. of the battery is 6.0 V. The potential difference (p.d.) across the thermistor is 1.5 V. The current in the circuit is 0.015 A.

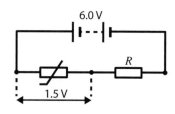

i Show that the p.d. across the fixed resistor is 4.5 V.

[1]

ii Calculate the resistance R of the fixed resistor.

TIP
The current in a series circuit is the same.

R = ... Ω   [3]

b What is the main reason for the total current entering a junction being equal to the sum of the currents leaving that same junction? Circle your answer.

A Charge is conserved.   **C** Potential difference is conserved.

B Energy is conserved.   **D** Electricity is conserved.   [1]

c This question is about the circuit opposite. The values of the resistors and the current in one of the resistors are shown on the circuit diagram.

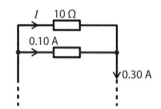

i Determine the current I in the 10 Ω resistor.

$I =$.. A   [1]

ii Calculate the p.d. across the parallel combination. Explain your answer.

p.d. =.. V   [3]

Action and use of circuit components

Student's Book pages 273–278 | Syllabus learning objectives 4.3.3.1;
SUPPLEMENT 4.3.3.2–4.3.3.3

···

1 A simple circuit is constructed by a student. The circuit has three resistors of the values shown in the circuit diagram. The resistors are connected in series to a battery.

The current in the circuit is 0.10 A.

The potential difference (p.d.) V across a resistor can be calculated using the equation: $V = IR$, where I is the current and R is the resistance.

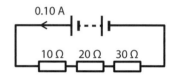

a Calculate the p.d. V across each resistor.

V across the 10 Ω resistor =.. V

V across the 20 Ω resistor =.. V

V across the 30 Ω resistor =.. V   [3]

b Complete the sentence below about this circuit.

For a constant current, the p.d. across an electrical conductor increases as its resistance

....   [1]

2 A potential divider circuit consists of a variable resistor and a fixed
SUPPLEMENT resistor of resistance 120 Ω. The maximum resistance of the variable resistor is 120 Ω and its minimum resistance is zero. The total p.d. across the circuit is 6.0 V.

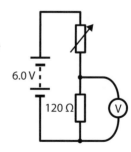

a State the reading on the voltmeter when the variable resistor has zero resistance.

voltmeter reading =.. V   [1]

b   Explain why the voltmeter reading will be 3.0 V when the variable resistor has maximum resistance.

....

.... [2]

c   For this circuit, circle all possible readings of the voltmeter.

   0.50 V   2.8 V   4.5 V   5.0 V   5.8 V   [1]

3 A potential divider circuit consisting of a thermistor is shown opposite. The resistance of the thermistor decreases as its temperature increases. The d.c. power supply has e.m.f. of 6.0 V and the fixed resistor has resistance 100 Ω.

PPLEMENT

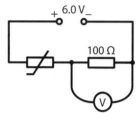

The thermistor is initially cold. It is then slowly warmed up.

a   Explain what happens to the current in the circuit.

....

.... [2]

b   Explain what happens to the voltmeter reading.

....

.... [2]

c   At one instant, the voltmeter reading is 2.5 V.

Use the potential divider equation $\dfrac{R_1}{R_2} = \dfrac{V_1}{V_2}$ to calculate the resistance R of the thermistor.

$R =$ .... Ω   [2]

d   At another instant, the resistance of the thermistor is 60 Ω.

Use the following potential divider equation $V_{out} = \dfrac{R_2}{R_1 + R_2} \times V_0$ to calculate the voltmeter reading.

voltmeter reading = ... V   [2]

Electrical safety

Student's Book pages 284–288 | Syllabus learning objectives 4.4.1–4.4.5

....

1 In many countries the mains voltage is between 120 V and 230 V. Any contact with such high voltages can be extremely dangerous.

a State why it may be sensible to have light switches outside a bathroom.

.... [1]

b Explain the danger of having an appliance cable as shown opposite.

....

.... [2]

c Explain why it may not be sensible to use a very thin cable for an electric kettle.

....

.... [2]

d What is the likely risk of using too many appliances connected to an extension cable? Give a reason for your answer.

....

.... [2]

2 A mains plug will always have a fuse inside. It is important that the fuse has the correct rating.

a Explain the purpose of a fuse.

....

.... [2]

b The diagram shows part of the label for an electric kettle.

LISTED 8H45
TYPE K15 KETTLE
120 V - 60 Hz 1500 W

i Determine the operating current for this kettle.

current = ... A   [3]

ii Which of the following fuses would be suitable in the plug of the electric kettle? Give a reason for your answer.

5.0 A   13 A   20 A

....

....   [2]

3 A fuse wire is an important safety device in a mains plug.

Here are five **incorrectly** sequenced statements about the operation of a fuse.

1. A fault occurs in the appliance.

2. The appliance switches off.

3. The fuse wire melts.

4. The fuse breaks the live connection to the appliance.

5. There is a large current in the fuse wire.

Place the statement numbers in the correct sequence.

....   [1]

4 **a** This question is about an appliance connected to the mains supply by a cable.

i One of the wires within the cable is known as the earth wire. Name the other two wires within the cable.

....   [1]

115

ii The appliance is a double-insulated appliance. It has two layers of insulation (plastic) surrounding the live wire. State why the earth wire does not need to be connected to the plug for this appliance.

....

.... [2]

iii Which wire in the cable appliance is connected to the external switch? Give a reason for your answer.

....

.... [2]

b A row of trip switches in a building are shown opposite.

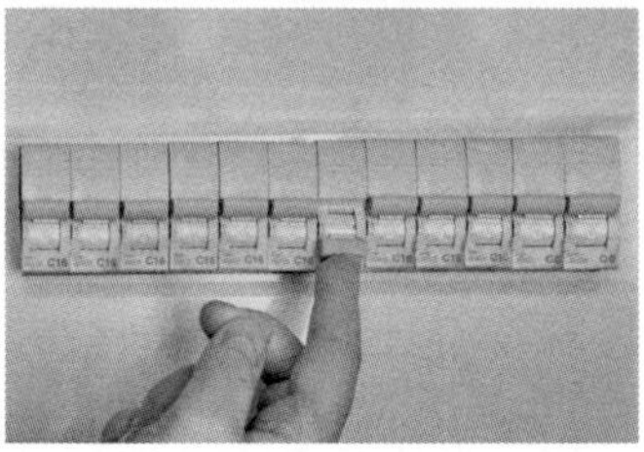

Which statement below applies to a trip switch?
Circle your answer.

A It is a circuit that sounds an alarm when the current is too large.

B It is a device that switches off when there is excessive current.

C It is a short length of wire that melts when the current is too large.

D It is a simple on-off mechanical switch. [1]

c An appliance with a metal casing has the earth connection to the metal case snapped off. Describe why this would be dangerous to the user when the live wire accidently touches the casing.

....

.... [2]

Electromagnetic induction

Student's Book pages 292–296 | Syllabus learning objectives 4.5.1.1–4.5.1.3;
SUPPLEMENT 4.5.1.4–4.5.1.5; 4.5.2.1–4.5.2.2

1 Complete the sentence below.

A conductor .... across a magnetic field, or a ....

magnetic field linking with a conductor, can induce an electromotive force (e.m.f.) in the

conductor.   [2]

2 Put simply, electromagnetic induction refers to generating, or inducing, an electromotive force (e.m.f.) in a conductor using magnetism.

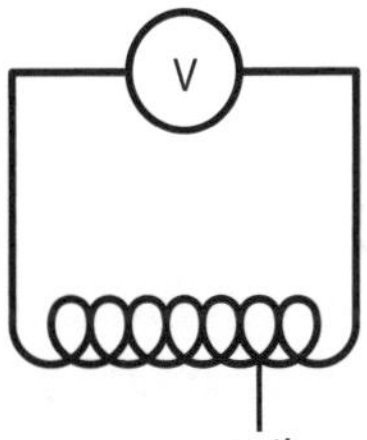

A wire coil is connected to an analogue voltmeter, as shown in the diagram.

Place a tick ✓ in the last column if the experiment described will cause the voltmeter pointer to briefly deflect.

Experiment	Tick ✓ if there is induced e.m.f.
Holding a magnet stationary close to the coil.	
Moving a magnet towards the coil.	
Moving a magnet away from the coil.	
Moving the coil towards the magnet.	
Moving the coil away from the magnet.	
Switching on an electromagnet close to the coil.	
Switching off an electromagnet close to the coil.	

[7]

3 **a** A copper conductor is placed between the poles of a horseshoe magnet. The wire is moved vertically upwards. The ammeter shows a deflection indicating a current flow because of the induced e.m.f. across the ends of the conductor.

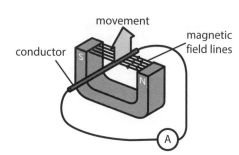

State two ways, in which the magnitude of the induced e.m.f. can be increased.

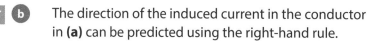

[2]

b The direction of the induced current in the conductor in **(a)** can be predicted using the right-hand rule.

On the diagram opposite, indicate which fingers and thumb give the direction of the magnetic field (use letter F), the direction of the induced current (use the letter C) and the direction of the motion or force (use the letter M).

[1]

c A strong magnet is dropped vertically. It first falls through a flat coil X at the top and then through another flat coil Y at the bottom. Each coil is connected to an analogue voltmeter.

Which coil will produce the greater electromotive force? Give a reason for your answer.

X

Y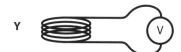

[2]

4 The diagram shows a bar magnet placed close to the axis of a coil of wire wrapped around an iron core. When the magnet is quickly pushed towards the end X of the coil, a current is induced in the coil such that the end X of the coil is a north-seeking (N) pole. These two like poles repel.

coil with soft-iron core

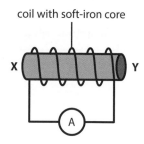

a Complete the sentence below.

The .... of an induced e.m.f. opposes the change causing it. [1]

b The magnet is pulled away from the end X of the coil.

   i State what happens to the direction of the induced current in the coil.

.... [1]

   ii Suggest the polarity of the end X of the coil when the current is induced in the coil. You may find your answer to **(a)** helpful.

.... [1]

5 **a** A simple alternating current (a.c.) generator consists of a coil rotating in a magnetic field provided by a permanent magnet.

SUPPLEMENT

The table below has some statements, that may or may not be correct for an a.c. generator.

Place a tick ✓ in the last column if the statement is correct and applicable to the generator.

Statement	Place a tick ✓ here if correct ...
Rotating the coil faster will increase the maximum output e.m.f.	
Rotating the coil slower or faster does not change the output frequency.	
The generator provides a constant output e.m.f.	
The generator uses commutators and brushes.	
The generator uses slip rings and brushes.	
Using a stronger magnetic field has no effect on the output e.m.f.	

[6]

b The diagram shows the coil of a generator rotating in a magnetic field. The magnetic field may be considered to be uniform between the north-seeking (N) and south-seeking (S) poles.

The graph on the left-hand side of the diagram shows the variation with time of the electromotive force (e.m.f.) from this a.c. generator.

On the graph above, mark all the times at which the plane of the coil is:

- parallel to the magnetic field using the letter P

- at right angles to the magnetic field using the letter R.   [2]

Magnetic effect of current

Student's Book pages 297–301 | Syllabus learning objectives 4.5.3.1–4.5.3.3;
SUPPLEMENT 4.5.3.4–4.5.3.5

1 A student is given the task of mapping out the magnetic field pattern for a current-carrying wire using a plotting compass. The diagram below shows the current-carrying wire with the compass placed above and then below the wire.

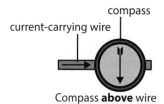
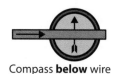

Compass **above** wire   Compass **below** wire

a State the relative directions of the magnetic field at these two points.

                                                                              [1]

b The current-carrying wire is shown by a circle below. The wire is at right angles to the plane of the paper. Using at least three magnetic field lines, sketch the magnetic field pattern around the current-carrying wire.

                                                                              [3]

SUPPLEMENT c i State how the magnetic field strength of the magnetic field changes with distance from the centre of the wire.

.... [1]

ii The direction of the current is reversed, and the size of the current in the wire is also increased.

Describe how the magnetic field pattern would change.

....

.... [2]

2 A solenoid is a long length of coiled wire. The solenoid has a magnetic field that looks very much like that of a permanent magnet, except the magnetic field can be switched on or off.

The diagram below is the magnetic field pattern sketched by a student when using iron filings sprinkled on a flat card.

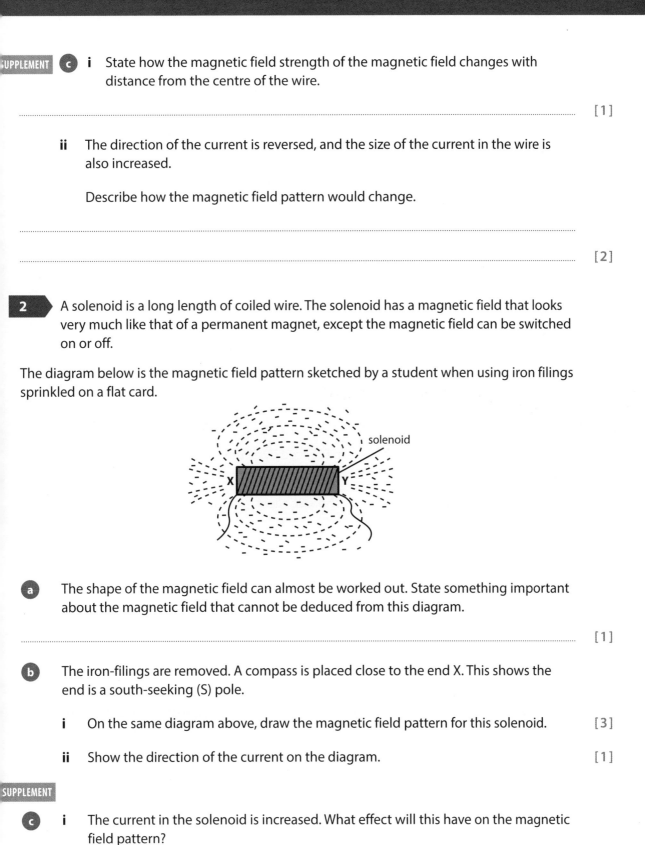

a The shape of the magnetic field can almost be worked out. State something important about the magnetic field that cannot be deduced from this diagram.

.... [1]

b The iron-filings are removed. A compass is placed close to the end X. This shows the end is a south-seeking (S) pole.

i On the same diagram above, draw the magnetic field pattern for this solenoid. [3]

ii Show the direction of the current on the diagram. [1]

SUPPLEMENT

c i The current in the solenoid is increased. What effect will this have on the magnetic field pattern?

.... [1]

ii The direction of the current in the solenoid is now reversed. What effect will this have on the magnetic field pattern?

.... [1]

• •

Force on current-carrying conductor and the d.c. motor

Student's Book pages 302–305 | Syllabus learning objectives 4.5.4.1;
SUPPLEMENT 4.5.4.2–4.5.4.3 ; 4.5.5.1; SUPPLEMENT 4.5.5.2

....

1 This question is about the force experienced by a current-carrying conductor.

a A teacher is demonstrating the force experienced by a current-carrying wire. Circle all the essential items necessary for the experiment.

battery   connecting wires   crocodile clips   horseshoe magnet

protractor   ruler   spring   thin copper wire

[3]

b Complete the sentence below.

A current-carrying wire will experience the largest force when it is placed

.... to the magnetic field. This wire has no force acting on it when

placed parallel to the magnetic field lines. [1]

c A current-carrying wire experiences a force to the **left** when placed in a magnetic field.

State the direction of the force on the wire when:

i the direction of the current is reversed

.... [1]

ii the direction of the field is reversed.

.... [1]

UPPLEMENT **d** A current-carrying wire is placed at right angles to a magnetic field. Determine the direction of the force on the wire in the two cases below.

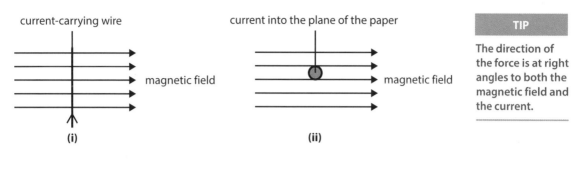

current-carrying wire

current into the plane of the paper

magnetic field

magnetic field

(i) **(ii)**

> **TIP**
>
> The direction of the force is at right angles to both the magnetic field and the current.

....

....

[2]

2 A beam of electrons in a vacuum travels through a region of a magnetic field. The directions of the magnetic field and electron flow are shown in the diagram opposite.

UPPLEMENT

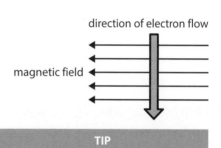

direction of electron flow

magnetic field

> **TIP**
>
> The direction of electron flow is in the opposite direction to conventional current.

What is the direction of the force experienced by the electrons? Circle your answer.

A Into the plane of the paper.   **C** To the left.

B Out of the plane of the paper.   **D** To the right.   [1]

3 The diagram below shows a loudspeaker.

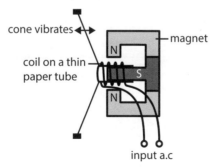

cone vibrates

magnet

coil on a thin paper tube

N

S

N

input a.c

a Connecting the coil of wire to a battery moves the paper cone away from the magnet.

State why the paper cone moves in the opposite direction when the same battery is connected with reverse polarity to the coil.

.... [1]

b Explain how connecting the coil to an alternating current will produce a sound with a specific note from the loudspeaker.

....

.... [2]

4 A relay is made from an electromagnetic coil and a magnetic switch. A light-operated relay circuit is shown opposite.

The resistance of the LDR decreases as the brightness of the light falling on it increases.

The LDR has a piece of black card on top. The resistance of the LDR is large. The potential difference across the relay coil is small, and as such is not magnetised enough to close the switch.

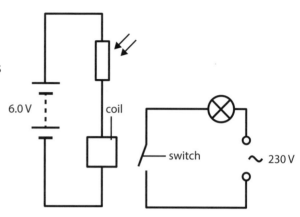

The card is now removed. Light shines on the LDR.

a State whether the p.d. across the coil is smaller, the same, or larger.

.... [1]

b Describe what happens to the circuit on the right-hand side.

....

.... [2]

5 A d.c. motor is connected to a cell. An incomplete diagram of a d.c. motor is shown below.

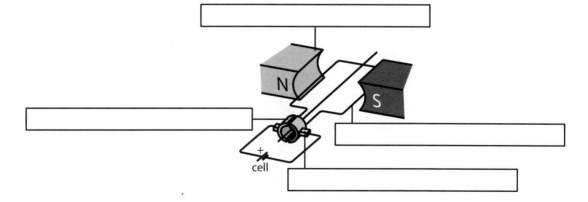

a Complete the diagram by identifying the four components of the d.c. motor. [4]

b State three factors that would affect the speed of rotation or the turning effect of the motor.

1. ....

2. ....

3. .... [3]

UPPLEMENT

c Explain why the motor coil will rotate anticlockwise.

....

.... [2]

UPPLEMENT

d Explain how the continuous rotation of the motor coil is made possible by one of the components.

....

.... [2]

• •

Transformers

Student's Book pages 305–309 | Syllabus learning objectives 4.5.6.1–4.5.6.5;
SUPPLEMENT 4.5.6.6–4.5.6.7

....

1 This question is about a simple transformer.

a You are given a soft-iron core and insulated copper wire. Describe how you can make a simple transformer.

....

....

.... [3]

b Complete the sentence below.

The input coil of a transformer is called the .... coil, and the

output coil is called the .... coil. [1]

c A diagram of simple transformer is shown opposite. A transformer
can either be step-down or step-up.

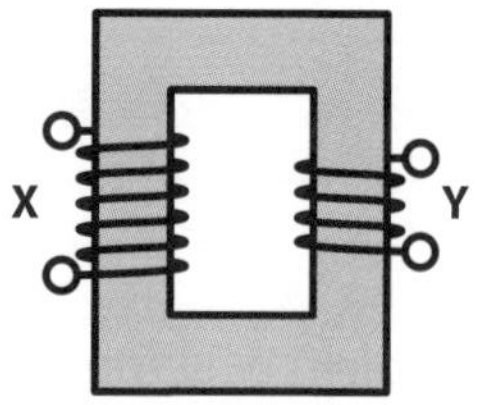

i What type of transformer would you get when X is the input
and Y is the output? Give a reason for your answer.

....

.... [2]

ii What type of transformer would you get when Y is the input and X is the output?
Give a reason for your answer.

....

.... [2]

2 The transmission of power using overhead cables happens at high-voltage. At a power
station, a step-up transformer is used to increase the alternating voltage from 12 kV to
400 kV for the transmission cables.

a Write an equation for turn-ratio equation for a step-up transformer using the terms
V_p, V_s, N_p and N_s.

[1]

b The input coil of the transformer has 200 turns. Calculate the number of turns N_s on the
output coil.

TIP
For a step-up transformer, $N_s > N_p$. This is a quick way to check your answer.

$N_s =$ .... [2]

SUPPLEMENT **c** Power loss in the overhead cables is minimised by having high voltage when transmitting a given power.

In the table below, place a tick ✓ in the last column if the statement is correct.

Statement	Place a tick ✓ here if correct ...
The current in the cable is very large.	
The current in the cables is smaller.	
The current in the overhead cable is direct current (d.c.).	
The power loss in a given cable is proportional to current	
The power loss is a given cable is proportional to current^2.	

[4]

3 The transformer of a mobile (cell) phone charger changes the mains voltage of 120 V to a supply of 9.0 V for the phone. The charging current for the phone is 1.8 A.

SUPPLEMENT

a Calculate the ratio $\dfrac{\text{number of turns on the primary coil}}{\text{number of turns on the secondary coil}}$.

ratio = ... [2]

b Calculate the current in the primary coil. State an assumption made in the calculation.

current =... A

Assumption: .... [4]

c Explain the principle of operation of the transformer. You may find the terms listed below helpful in your description.

- magnetic field

- induce e.m.f

- links

- soft-iron core

....

....

....

.... [3]

The atom

Student's Book pages 320–323 | Syllabus learning objectives 5.1.1.1–5.1.1.2;
SUPPLEMENT 5.1.1.3

··

1 The diagram opposite shows the basic structure of a neutral atom.

Two particles of the atom are labelled as A and B.

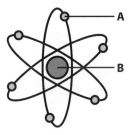

State the name of each particle and the type of charge it has.

Name of A: .... Charge on A: ....

Name of B: .... Charge on B: ....

2 Neutral atoms can be made into positive ions by removing electrons or negative ions by adding electrons.

A neutral atom, has electrons added and removed from it.

State the charge (positive or negative) of the resulting ion after the following step.

a two electrons are added to the atom and one removed.

charge on ion: .... [1]

b three electrons are added to the atom and five removed.

charge on ion: .... [1]

c four electrons are added to the atom and two are removed.

charge on ion: .... [1]

3 A beam of alpha (a) particles from a radioactive source are fired into a thin gold foil. The majority of the a particles went straight though the foil without any scattering or deflection. Some of the a particles were scattered through large angles, with some even 'back scattered'.

SUPPLEMENT

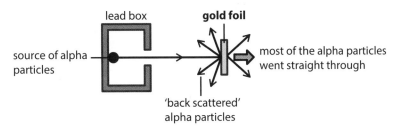

lead box   **gold foil**

source of alpha particles

most of the alpha particles went straight through

'back scattered' alpha particles

a The a particles have a positive charge. Which is the correct explanation for the deflection of the a particles? Circle your answer.

A The a particles bouncing off the solid gold sheet.

B The a particles repelling each other.

C The attraction between the electrons and the a particles.

D The repulsion between the positive nuclei and the a particles. [1]

b State what can be deduced from the fact that most of the a particles went straight though the foil without any deflection.

.... [1]

c The table below has some statements. Place a tick ✓ in the last column if the statement is correct for the nucleus of an atom.

Statement	Place a tick ✓ here if correct …
It has most of the mass of the atom.	
It has a positive charge.	
It is electrically neutral.	
It is extremely small compared with the size of the atom.	
It is made up of electrons.	
It is mainly a vacuum (empty space).	

[6]

The nucleus

Student's Book pages 323–326 | Syllabus learning objectives 5.1.2.1–5.1.2.5;
SUPPLEMENT 5.1.2.6–5.1.2.8

....

1 A particular nuclide can be represented by the notation $^{A}_{Z}X$.

a State what each letter in this notation represents.

X: .... [1]

A: .... [1]

Z: .... [1]

b The relative charge of the proton as +1. State the relative charges of the electron and of the neutron.

....

.... [2]

c Explain what is meant by an isotope.

.... [1]

d Here are some nuclides.

$^{90}_{38}Sr$ $\qquad$ $^{13}_{6}C$ $\qquad$ $^{238}_{92}U$ $\qquad$ $^{233}_{93}Np$ $\qquad$ $^{4}_{2}He$ $\qquad$ $^{11}_{6}C$

i Identify the nuclide with the largest number of neutrons. Explain your answer.

....

.... [2]

ii Identify two isotopes of an element.

.... [1]

iii State which neutral atom of the nuclides in this list will have the least number of orbiting electrons. Give a reason for your answer.

....

.... [2]

iv The nucleus of strontium $^{90}_{38}$ Sr is involved in a nuclear reaction. The nucleus absorbs a single neutron. Write down the nuclide notation for the newly formed nucleus. Explain your answer.

....

.... [2]

2 **SUPPLEMENT** The mass of the neutron is approximately the same as the mass of a proton. The relative mass of each of these particles is taken as 1. The relative charge of the proton is +1 and the relative charge of the neutron is 0.

Complete the table below by determining the approximate relative mass and relative charge of each nuclide.

Nuclide	Relative mass	Relative charge
$^{3}_{1}$ H		
$^{4}_{2}$ He		
$^{14}_{7}$ N		
$^{55}_{25}$ Mn		
$^{110}_{48}$ Cd		
$^{206}_{82}$ Pb		

[6]

3 **SUPPLEMENT** This question is about nuclear fission.

One of the many nuclear reactions taking place inside the core of a nuclear fission reactor is shown below.

$$^{235}_{92} U + {}^{1}_{0} n \rightarrow {}^{140}_{54} Xe + {}^{94}_{38} Sr + 2{}^{1}_{0} n$$

a What happens to the nucleus of uranium when it absorbs a neutron?

....

.... [2]

b State how the total mass of the particles after the fission reaction compares with the total mass of the particles before the reaction.

.... [1]

c State what is released as a consequence of the change in the mass during a fission reaction.

.... [1]

d Which two events take place in **both** fission and fusion reactions? Circle your answer.

A Energy is released and mass increases.

B Energy is released and mass decreases.

C High temperature and energy is released.

D High temperature and high pressure. [1]

4 This question is about nuclear fusion.

UPPLEMENT

One of the many nuclear reactions taking place inside the core of the Sun is shown below.

$$^{2}_{1}H + {}^{3}_{1}H \rightarrow {}^{4}_{2}He + {}^{1}_{0}n$$

a Complete the sentences below.

A fusion reaction is the .... of two nuclei. In this process,

there is a decrease in the .... and energy

is ....

b In the reaction in **(a)**, show that total relative charge before the reaction is equal to the total relative charge after the reaction.

[2]

Radioactivity

Student's Book pages 329–334 | Syllabus learning objectives 5.2.1.1–5.2.1.4; SUPPLEMENT 5.2.1.5 ; 5.2.2.1–5.2.2.2; SUPPLEMENT 5.2.2.3–5.2.2.4

1 This question is about the background radiation.

a Explain what is meant by the background radiation and name two main contributors to this radiation.

....

....　[3]

b Describe how the background count rate can be determined in the laboratory.

....

....

....　[3]

c In an experiment to determine the background count rate in the classroom, 20 counts are detected in 2.5 minutes.

Calculate the background count rate in counts per minute and in counts per second.

count rate = ... counts/min　[1]

count rate = ... counts/s　[2]

d A radiation detector (GM tube) is placed in front a radioactive source. A total of 120 counts are detected in a time of 80 s. Using your answer in **(c)**, calculate the corrected count rate in counts per minute.

corrected count rate =... counts/min   [3]

2 This question is about the three types of nuclear radiation – alpha radiation, beta radiation and gamma radiation.

a What symbols can you use instead of the names alpha, beta and gamma?

....   [1]

b All three nuclear radiations are often referred to as 'ionising' radiations because they will ionise the atoms of the matter through which they travel.

Which particle is **removed** from an atom during ionisation? Circle your answer.

A   electron   **B**   ion   **C**   neutron   **D**   proton   [1]

c The diagram below shows the penetration of the alpha, beta and gamma radiations through different materials (paper, aluminium and lead).

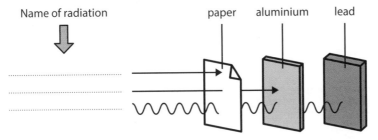

On the diagram, identify each type of radiation.   [3]

d Here are some bullet points written by a student related to one specific type of radiation.

- The radiation consists of particles.

- Each particle is a helium nucleus.

- Each particle has a relative charge of + 2.

Identify the type of the radiation.

....   [1]

e Name the radiation that is short-wavelength electromagnetic radiation, and has no charge.

.... [1]

f Name the radiation that is neither the one identified in **(d)** nor the one in **(e)**. Describe the nature of this radiation.

....

.... [3].

g List the three ionising radiations in the order of **decreasing** ionising ability.

most ionising   least ionising

.... [1]

3 The nuclear radiation emitted by radioactive sources are described as being *random* and *spontaneous*.

Explain what is meant by:

a random

.... [1]

b spontaneous.

.... [1]

4 Why do alpha-particles cause more ionisation than beta-particles travelling at the same

SUPPLEMENT speed through a given material? Circle your answer.

A The alpha-particles have greater kinetic energy and greater charge.

B The alpha-particles have less kinetic energy and greater charge.

C The beta-particles have greater kinetic energy and less charge.

D The beta-particles have the same kinetic energy and less charge. [1]

5

SUPPLEMENT

The identity of the radiation being emitted by a radioactive source can be confirmed by the way it travels through either magnetic or electric field.

a Which nuclear radiation is unaffected by both electric field and magnetic field? Give a reason for your answer.

.... [1]

b A beam of alpha-particles from a radioactive source travel through the electric field region between two oppositely charged plates; see the diagram opposite. The plates are in a vacuum.

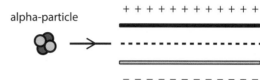

alpha-particle

i Explain the deflection of the alpha-particles between the plates.

....

.... [2]

ii On the diagram, show the likely path of the alpha-particles. [1]

c In **(b)**, the beam is replaced by beta-particles from a different source. Explain why the deflection of these particles will be opposite to that of the alpha-particles.

....

.... [2]

6

SUPPLEMENT

The diagram opposite shows the direction of travel of an alpha-particle and a beta-particle in a magnetic field. The direction of the magnetic field is into the plane of the paper.

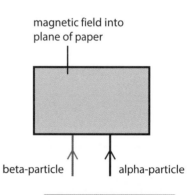

magnetic field into plane of paper

beta-particle   alpha-particle

Which of the following is correct about the deflection of these two particles? Circle your answer.

	Force on alpha-particle	Force on the beta-particle
A	left	left
B	left	right
C	right	left
D	right	right

TIP

You can use the left-hand rule to determine the direction of the force on the particle as it enters the region of magnetic field.

[1]

137

Radioactive decay

Student's Book pages 335–337 | Syllabus learning objectives 5.2.3.1–5.2.3.2;
SUPPLEMENT 5.2.3.3–5.2.3.5

....

1 ▸ Many smoke alarms have a small amount of the radioactive element americium. Americium nuclei decay randomly and spontaneously by emitting alpha-particles.

a State why, after many years, the source of americium in a smoke alarm will no longer just have americium nuclei.

.... [1]

b What is the main reason for the decay of the americium nuclei? Circle your answer.

A They are affected by temperature.

C They behave randomly.

D They behave spontaneously. [1]

B They are unstable nuclei.

2 ▸ A geologist digs out a sample of rock that has many different types of radioactive nuclei. The rock emits all three types of nuclear radiations.

a Name two emissions that consists of particles.

.... [1]

b Name one type of emission that has no charge.

.... [1]

3 ▸ The table below shows some data on the isotopes beryllium (Be).

Isotope	$^{9}_{4}Be$	$^{10}_{4}Be$	$^{11}_{4}Be$	$^{12}_{4}Be$
Decay mode	Stable	β	β	β

a Explain why some isotopes of beryllium may be radioactive.

....

.... [2]

b A beryllium nucleus will transform into a nucleus of boron (B) after a beta emission.

i Complete the decay equation below for $^{10}_{4}Be$.

$$^{10}_{4}Be \rightarrow {}^{0}_{-1}\beta + \text{............} B$$

[2]

ii Explain what change occurs within the nuclide of $^{10}_{4}Be$ during β-emission.

....

.... [2]

4 **a** Complete the sentences below about radioactive emissions.

There is no change in the element during the emission of ....
radiation. In both .... decay and ....
decay, the nuclei transform into different elements. [2]

b In alpha decay of a nuclide, explain the:

i change in the nucleon number and the proton number

....

.... [2]

ii effect of this decay on the nucleus of the atom.

....

.... [2]

c In beta decay of a nuclide, explain the change in the nucleon number and the proton number.

....

.... [2]

d Complete the following nuclear decays.

TIP
In each decay, the nucleon and protons numbers must 'balance' on both sides.

i $^{240}_{94}Pu \rightarrow {}^{4}_{2}He + \text{............} U$ [2]

ii $\text{............} W \rightarrow {}^{4}_{2}He + {}^{174}_{72}Hf$ [2]

iii $\text{............} H \rightarrow {}^{0}_{-1}\beta + {}^{3}_{2}He$ [2]

Half-life, uses of radioactivity and safety

Student's Book pages 337–344 | Syllabus learning objectives 5.2.4.1; SUPPLEMENT 5.2.4.2–5.2.4.3 ; 5.2.5.1– 5.2.5.2; SUPPLEMENT 5.2.5.3

....

1 This question is about half-life.

a Define the half-life of an isotope.

.... [1]

b Use the tables below to estimate the half-life of the isotope to the nearest day in **(i)** and to the nearest year in **(ii)**. Show any supporting calculations.

i

Number of undecayed nuclei	2000	1580	1270	998	803
Time /days	0	1.0	2.0	3.0	4.0

half-life =.. days   [2]

ii

Count rate / min	820	405	202	100	49
Time / years	0	2.0	4.0	6.0	8.0

half-life =.. years   [2]

c The half-life of the isotope of sulfur $^{37}_{16}$S is 5.0 minutes.

At time $t = 0$, there are 1000 nuclei of this isotope in a sample.

i Complete the table below. [2]

t / min	N
0	1000
5	
10	
15	
20	

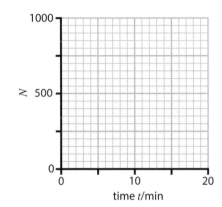

TIP

Plot carefully and use a thin pencil to draw a smooth curve.

ii Sketch a graph of number of undecayed nuclei N against time t next to the table. [3]

2

A Geiger–Müller tube and a counter are used to determine the background count rate in the laboratory. The average value for the background count rate is found to be 10 counts per minute.

A scientist determines the **total** count rate from a weak beta-emitting source at regular intervals. The table below shows the data collected.

Time / s	30	60	90	120	150
Count rate per minute	52	40	31	25	21
Corrected count rate per minute					

a Without taking account of the background radiation, show that the **incorrect** value for the half-life of the isotope of the source would be about 90 s.

[2]

b Complete the last row of the table. [1]

c Use the corrected count rate to determine the half-life of the isotope.

half-life =.. s [2]

3

SUPPLEMENT

The diagram opposite shows the inside of a domestic smoke alarm. The radioactive source is often alpha-emitting americium-241. The source, and the electronics, are housed in a plastic case. The alarm is usually located on the ceiling of a room or a hallway.

a Suggest why an alpha-emitting source would not be harmful to people coming close to the alarm.

.... [1]

b Suggest how the long half-life of americium-241 of 430 years makes it suitable for domestic smoke alarms.

.... [1]

4 **a** A paper mill uses a radioactive source for monitoring and controlling the thickness of paper. The isotope of the source has a very long half-life so that it does not need to be changed often.

Explain why a beta-emitting source is used and not alpha or gamma emitters.

....

....

....

.... [3]

b State the type of nuclear radiation that can be used for irradiating food to kill bacteria and sterilising medical equipment.

.... [1]

5 This question is about the precautions employed when using ionising radiations.

a In the school laboratory, radioactive sources are locked away and stored in lead-lined boxes. Explain why lead is a suitable material for shielding.

....

.... [2]

b All ionising radiations cause serious damage to cells in living things. State two consequences of damaged cells on people.

....

.... [2]

c Suggest why it would be safe to hold an alpha-emitting source in a long-handled tong while keeping the source at arm's length.

....

.... [2]

SUPPLEMENT **d** A radiographer works regularly with beta and gamma sources in a hospital.

The table below has some statements. Place a tick ✓ in the last column if the statement is a relevant precaution for the radiographer.

Statement	Place a tick ✓ here if correct …
Increase the exposure time with the radioactive sources.	
Keep the sources close by you.	
Keep the sources locked away and bring them out only when needed.	
Keep your distance from the radioactive sources.	
Wear a lead-lined apron.	
Wear a normal cotton apron.	

[6]

Solar System

Student's Book pages 354–361 | Syllabus learning objectives 6.1.1.1–6.1.1.3; 6.1.2.1–6.1.2.2; SUPPLEMENT 6.1.2.7

1 This question is about the Earth and the Moon.

a Explain the simple observation that the Sun rises in the east and then after approximately 12 hours it sets in the west.

....

.... [2]

b Explain why we have periodic seasons of summers and winters.

....

....

.... [3]

c The Moon's cycle of phases can be used to estimate the time it takes for the Moon to orbit once around the Earth.

The diagram below the phases of the Moon over a period of 14 days.

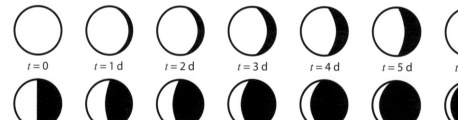

$t = 0$ $t = 1\,d$ $t = 2\,d$ $t = 3\,d$ $t = 4\,d$ $t = 5\,d$ $t = 6\,d$

$t = 7\,d$ $t = 8\,d$ $t = 9\,d$ $t = 10\,d$ $t = 11\,d$ $t = 12\,d$ $t = 13\,d$

$t = 14\,d$

i In the space provided below, draw the relative positions of the Sun, Moon and the Earth for the 'full-Moon' phase at time $t = 0$.

[2]

    ii   Use the phases diagram to estimate the orbital period of the Moon.

orbital period = ... days   **[1]**

2   This question is about the Solar System.

a   Name the four planets that orbit the closest to the Sun.

....   **[1]**

b   Name the four planets that orbit the farthest from the Sun.

....   **[1]**

c   Describe how the structure (size and composition) of the planets mentioned in **(a)** differ from the planets mentioned in **(b)**.

....

....   **[2]**

d   Here is a list of terms that **may** be the answers to the questions that follow.

asteroid belt	comet	Jupiter	Mars
Mercury	natural satellite	Neptune	Pluto

    i   Comets are categorised as smaller Solar System bodies **(SSSB)**. Name another object in the Solar System in this category.

....   **[1]**

    ii   Name a dwarf planet.

....   **[1]**

    iii   Name the two planets between which most of the objects in the asteroid belt are located.

....   **[1]**

    iv   Name an object that leaves a gaseous tail as it gets closer to the Sun.

....   **[1]**

    v   Where are some of the minor planets located in the Solar System?

....   **[1]**

vi Name a natural object that orbits around a planet.

.... [1]

vii Comets tend to have more elliptical orbits than the eight planets in the Solar System. The diagram below shows such an elliptical orbit.

Mark the position of the Sun on this diagram. [1]

3 The accretion model describes the creation of the Solar System. The attractive gravitational force plays a key part in the creation of the Solar System.

The statements below are roughly in sequence, and show the formation of the Solar System.

Complete the sentences using **some** of the words listed below. [7]

asteroid	comets	disc	dust	dwarf	five	four	gas

giant	ice	Pluto	sphere	Sun

- Gravitational pull starts to gather and rotate .... and .... cloud.

- The rotation creates a .... with a bulge at the centre.

- The bulging centre of the disc was hot and formed the ....

- Lighter elements closer to the centre were gathered by the Sun.

- Heavier elements (iron, silicon, aluminium, zinc, etc.) remained close to the centre. This material spiralled and joined together to the .... inner-rocky planets.

- Lighter gases (hydrogen, helium, methane, etc) spiralled and formed the four outer-gaseous .... planets.

- Left-over material between the Sun and Jupiter formed the objects within the .... belt.

- Far-flung material from the Sun was cold and icy. .... originate from outer reaches of the Solar System.

Analysis of the Solar System

Student's Book pages 362–365 | Syllabus learning objectives SUPPLEMENT 6.1.1.4 ;
6.1.2.3–6.1.2.6; SUPPLEMENT 6.1.2.8– 6.1.2.10

··

1 Here are some facts about Jupiter written by a student.

• It is the most massive planet in the Solar System.

• It has mass that is about 2.5 times the total mass of all the planets in the Solar System.

• The mass of the Sun is more than 1000 times the mass of Jupiter.

Suggest why the planets in the Solar System orbit the Sun.

.... [1]

2 The total energy of a planet orbiting the Sun is conserved.

SUPPLEMENT

a State the two types of energy stores for an orbiting planet.

.... [1]

b The diagram below shows a planet orbiting the Sun in an elliptical orbit.

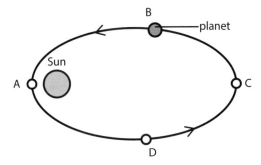

At which point **A**, **B**, **C** or **D** will the planet have the **least** kinetic energy? Circle your
answer on the diagram above. [1]

3 **a**   This question is about the gravitational field around a planet.

Describe **two** factors that influence the strength of the gravitational field around a planet.

....

....

....

.... [4]

SUPPLEMENT

b   The attractive gravitational force on the planet from the Sun is responsible for the motion of a planet in its orbit.

Describe how the orbital speed experienced by the planet depends on the gravitational field strength due the Sun.

....

.... [2]

4   The speed of light in a vacuum is 3.0×10^8 m/s.

Calculate the time it takes for light to travel from Mars to the Earth when the distance between them is 78 million km.

TIP
You need to convert the distance into metres (m).

time = ... s   [3]

5 You will be doing some analysis on the Solar System based on the information given in this table.

SUPPLEMENT

Planet	Mass/ 10^{24} kg	Mean orbital distance from Sun/10^6 km	Closest distance to Sun/ 10^6 km	Furthest distance from the Sun/ 10^6 km	Orbital duration or period/ Earth days	Mean surface temperature/°C	Density/ kg/m^3	Surface gravitational field strength/ N/kg
Mercury	0.33	57.9	46.0	69.8	88.0	167	5427	3.7
Venus	4.87	108.2	107.5	108.9	224.7	464	5243	8.9
Earth	5.97	149.6	147.1	152.1	365.2	15	5514	9.8
Mars	0.64	227.9	206.6	249.2	687.0	−65	3933	3.7
Jupiter	1900	778.6	740.5	816.6	4331	−110	1326	23.1
Saturn	570	1433.5	1352.6	1514.5	10 747	−140	687	9.0
Uranus	87	2872.5	2741.3	3003.6	30 589	−195	1271	8.7
Neptune	100	4495.1	4444.5	4545.7	59 800	−200	1638	11.0

a State one reason for Jupiter having the largest value for the surface gravitational field strength.

.... [1]

b Apart from the planet Venus (which is shrouded in a thick layer of carbon dioxide), explain the general trend of the variation of the mean surface temperature of planets.

....

.... [2]

c The density of rocks found on the Earth is about 5000 kg/m^3. What can you deduce about the composition of the four inner planets?

.... [1]

d How can you deduce from the data above that all planets have elliptical orbits rather than circular orbits?

.... [1]

e The orbital speed v of a planet can be calculated using the equation $v = \dfrac{2\pi r}{T}$

i State what r and T represent.

.... [1]

ii Calculate the orbital speed v in m/s of the planets Mars and Neptune.

TIP
1 day $= 24 \times 3600 = 86\,400$ s

v (**Mars**) =.. m/s [3]

v (**Neptune**) =.. m/s [3]

iii Complete the sentence below.

Neptune has a .... speed than Mars as it

is .... away from the Sun. [1]

• •

Stars and the light-year

Student's Book pages 370–376 | Syllabus learning objectives 6.2.1.1;
SUPPLEMENT 6.2.1.2 ; 6.2.2.1; SUPPLEMENT 6.2.2.2–6.2.2.3

1 **a** Describe what is meant by the Milky Way.

....

.... [2]

b List the following objects in the order of **increasing** distance from the Earth.

Andromeda galaxy   Moon   Star   Sun

.... [1]

c The Sun is a typical medium size star.

i The nuclei of the Sun are mainly made from two elements.

Name these elements.

.... [2]

ii The Sun radiates its energy in the form of electromagnetic radiation. In the list below, circle the three regions of the electromagnetic radiation where it emits most of its energy.

radio waves   infrared   visible   ultraviolet   X-rays   [1]

PPLEMENT **iii** The Sun is stable star that radiates energy into space.

Describe how energy is produced in the Sun.

....

.... [2]

d The nearest star to the Sun is Proxima Centauri. It is about 4.25 light-years away.

i Define the term light-year (ly).

.... [1]

JPPLEMENT **ii** What is the distance of 1 light-year in metres (m)?

.... [1]

iii The speed of light in a vacuum is 3.0×10^8 m/s and 1 year $= 3.15 \times 10^7$ s. Calculate the distance of 4.25 ly in metres (m).

4.25 ly = ... m   [4]

iv Suggest why light-year is used to measure the distance of stars and galaxies.

.... [1]

v The centre of our galaxy is about 30 000 ly away. How long does it take for light to travel from the centre of the galaxy to us?

.... [1]

2

SUPPLEMENT

This question is about the formation and life cycle (evolution) of stars.

a Describe how a stable star is formed from an interstellar cloud of gas and dust that contains hydrogen.

....

....

....

....

.... [5]

b After which stage below will a star start to expand into a red giant or a red supergiant? Circle your answer.

A When a protostar is born.

B When a white dwarf is formed.

C When gravitational forces start bringing together the gas and dust cloud.

D When it runs out of the hydrogen necessary for nuclear reactions. [1]

c A supernova is a catastrophic event in which a star implodes rapidly.

What is created during this event that may be responsible for forming stars and planets in the future?

A black holes   **B** heavier elements   **C** radiation   **D** white dwarfs [1]

d Here is a list of some objects. Circle your answer.

black hole   neutron star   planetary nebula   red giant

red supergiant   star   supernova   white dwarf

Using the objects from this list, show the life cycle of a:

i low mass star (e.g Sun)

....

....

.... [3]

ii massive star.

....

....

.... [3]

• •

The Universe

Student's Book pages 377–380 | Syllabus learning objectives 6.2.3.1–6.2.3.4;
SUPPLEMENT 6.2.3.5–6.2.3.11

....

1 What is the approximate diameter of our galaxy (Milky Way)? Circle your answer.

A 1000 ly **B** 10 000 ly **C** 100 000 ly **D** 1000 000 ly [1]

2 It is estimated that there are 100 billion galaxies in the Universe. Each galaxy has about 100 billion stars.

TIP
1 billion is 1000 000 000 or 10^9

a Determine how many stars there are in the Universe.

number of stars =.. [2]

b The average mass of a star is about 2.0×10^{30} kg.

Estimate the total mass of matter in the Universe.

mass =.. kg [2]

3 **a** What does the term redshift of electromagnetic waves emitted by receding stars and galaxies mean? Circle your answer.

It represents the increase in the observed …

A amplitude **B** frequency **C** redness **D** wavelength.

[1]

b Complete the sentence below.

Redshift in the observed electromagnetic radiation from galaxies shows that they are all moving .... from each other; hence the Universe must be ....

[2]

4 The diagram opposite shows the spectrum of light from the Sun (which may be regarded as being stationary relative to the Earth) and the same spectrum from a distant galaxy. The 'lines' on the spectrum from the galaxy seem to be identical to that from the Sun, except they are all shifted to the right.

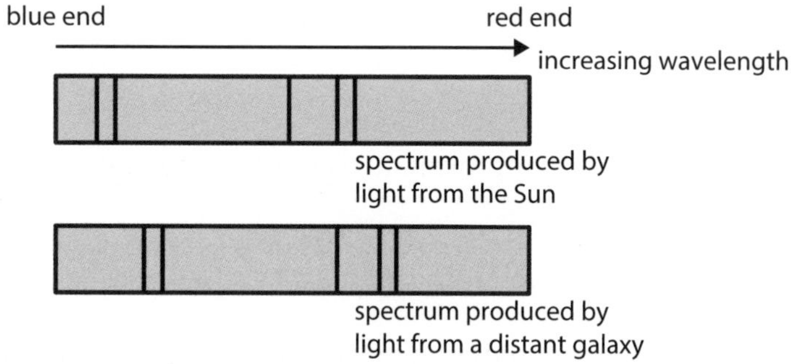

blue end → red end
increasing wavelength

spectrum produced by light from the Sun

spectrum produced by light from a distant galaxy

Explain the significance of the shifting of the spectrum.

....
....
....

[3]

5 **a** Explain the term Big Bang Theory and state two pieces of evidence that support this theory.

SUPPLEMENT

....
....
....

[3]

b Explain the term cosmic microwave background radiation (CMBR).

....
....

[2]

154

6 This question is about two distant galaxies.

PPLEMENT

a State how the receding speed v of a galaxy is determined from an observation carried out on the Earth.

....

.... [2]

b State the relationship between the recessional speed v of a galaxy and its distance d from the Earth.

.... [1]

c What objects are used in a distant galaxy to determine its distance from the Earth? Circle your answer.

A black hole   **C** supernova

B neutron star   **D** white dwarf   [1]

d The table below shows some data on two galaxies X and Y.

	v (km/s)	d (million ly)
Galaxy X	5000	240
Galaxy Y	1000	

Use the relationship you gave in **(b)** to determine the distance of the galaxy Y in million light-years (ly).

distance = ... million ly   [3]

7 **a** Define the Hubble constant H_0.

UPPLEMENT

.... [1]

b State the current estimated value of the Hubble constant H_0 and its unit.

$H_0 = $ .... unit: .... [2]

c Use your value of the Hubble constant to estimate the age in years of the Universe.

1 year $= 3.15 \times 10^7$ s

age = ... years   [3]

d How is your answer in **(c)** related to the Big Bang?

....   [1]